A·THOMPSON
UNIVERSITY OF GLAMORGAN
MAY 2000

KU-423-368

The Politics of Postmodernity

An Introduction to Contemporary Politics and Culture

John R. Gibbins and Bo Reimer

SAGE Publications
London · Thousand Oaks · New Delhi

© John R. Gibbins and Bo Reimer 1999

First published 1999

All rights reserved. No part of this publication may be
reproduced, stored in a retrieval system, transmitted
or utilized in any form or by any means, electronic,
mechanical, photocopying, recording or otherwise,
without permission in writing from the Publishers.

SAGE Publications Ltd
6 Bonhill Street
London EC2A 4PU

SAGE Publications Inc
2455 Teller Road
Thousand Oaks, California 91320

SAGE Publications India Pvt Ltd
32, M-Block Market
Greater Kailash - I
New Delhi 110 048

British Library Cataloguing in Publication data

A catalogue record for this book is
available from the British Library

ISBN 0 7619 5222 5
ISBN 0 7619 5223 3 (pbk)

Library of Congress catalog available

Typeset in Palatino by M Rules
Printed in Great Britain by Biddles Ltd,
Guildford, Surrey

Contents

Acknowledgements

We wish to thank the European Science Foundation for providing us with the opportunity to converse during participation in the Beliefs in Government Project (1989–1995), to Max Kaase and Ken Newton, the directors of the project, and to Jan Van Deth and Elinor Scarbrough, convenors of the Impact of Values working group. Support for John Gibbins also came from the Ferran Requejo, the doctoral students, Anita Noguera, Angel Guevara Casanovas, and the Facultat de Ciencies Socials i de la Communicacio, Pompeu Fabra University, Barcelona for the opportunities a visiting post gave, to draft chapters in Spring 1997. Thanks are due to the University of Teesside for the time and to its Centre for Social and Policy Research for encouragement. Bo Reimer wishes to express his gratitude to faculty and students at the Department of Communication, San José State University, as well as to colleagues at the Department of Journalism and Mass Communication, Göteborg University. A special thanks to Magnus Andersson, André Jansson and James Lull for stimulating discussions and valuable suggestions.

Introduction

This book is called *The Politics of Postmodernity*. A simpler, less ambitious title would have been *Politics in Postmodernity*. That title would not have been misleading since the main question we are addressing is this: *what happens to politics in postmodern times?* However, we would not have been completely satisfied with that title. It would have suggested that politics in postmodernity could be addressed and analysed without any need for reflecting about what postmodernity, and related concepts such as postmodernism and postmodernization, 'is' or could be. We do not think that is the case.

For us postmodernity signifies not only a specific historical period with particular forces, actions and relationships – which we will analyse in this book – but also a particular discourse. It signifies a particular way of looking at the world and of doing research. It also signifies a particular way of treating the relationship between, on the one hand, what we know and think, and, on the other hand, how we are able to express these things through language.

Thus, for us, analysing politics in, and in relation to, postmodernity means more than just analysing politics as such. It also, necessarily, means engaging in the politics of postmodernity. Therefore the title.

The book is structured as follows: we start with an analysis of the discourses of postmodernity, postmodernism and postmodernization (Chapter 1). This will give the reader our chosen perspective on the discourses. We then move to an analysis of politics in postmodernity. But as we see it, the way politics functions, and the ways people make use of politics, cannot be understood without placing politics in a larger framework. It needs to be contextualized: politics constitutes a specific sphere – the polity – with its own logic. However, even though it does constitute a specific sphere, it is still related to other spheres, to economic, social, technological and cultural spheres, for instance, and all of these spheres together make up the structures of postmodernity. Similarly, politics plays highly specific roles for people in everyday life, but in order to understand these roles, they have to be placed within the more general framework of everyday life; they are most meaningfully analysed by *first* focusing on how people generally act and make choices in everyday life, and *then* focusing on how politics fits into that pattern.

This means that before moving to the specifics of politics, we will outline some more general characteristics of postmodernity (Chapters 2–5). We will discuss the main processes in postmodernity and we will analyse how people make sense of everyday life in a postmodern age. In so doing, we will try to give the context within which politics functions, but we will also try to show how politics in postmodernity becomes more integrated with other everyday life practices. Thus, through contextualization we will question the traditional boundaries between the political and the non-political. We start with the macro-processes of postmodernity in Chapter 2, dealing primarily with globalization and with the notion of postmodernity as disorganized capitalism. In Chapter 3 we deal with the role of the mass media in postmodernity. That chapter is a bridge between the macro and the micro. In the following two chapters we then turn explicitly to the micro level and discuss self-identity and lifestyle in postmodernity.

The analysis of politics in postmodernity takes up three chapters. We first analyse the ways politics functions and is used in everyday life, and how this is changing in postmodernity. A particular emphasis is here put on the new social movements. We then turn to the question of the role of the state. Finally, we discuss what we see as the *postmodern progressive potential*. What will happen to politics when we are further into postmodernity? A postscript on the future of political science in postmodern times closes the book.

In this book the reader will find two arguments supporting the use of the notion of postmodernity. The first reason – the theoretical – we have already touched upon. But there is also an empirical reason. We believe that contemporary Western societies may meaningfully be analysed as postmodern societies. These societies are to a large degree shaped by a constellation of new forces. The processes of mediazation and globalization are becoming increasingly important, and contemporary (capitalist) societies are becoming increasingly complex, disorganized and unpredictable. This does not entail a complete break with modernity. As Hassan (1985) argues, history is a palimpsest, and our time contains traditional, modern and postmodern characteristics. All in all, however, the scope, the speed and the number of forces have increased to the extent that instead of modernity and modernization we prefer to speak of postmodernity and postmodernization. These forces shape everyday life in new ways, and this creates new possibilities and opportunities – as well as new problems.

We believe that structural changes are creating the material conditions for new ways of acting and feeling in postmodernity. The key notion that we introduce is the notion of *expressivism*. We believe that this notion more meaningfully than others captures the 'structure of feeling' (Williams 1961) that characterizes people's ambitions and wishes in postmodernity. Expressivism has evolved in a complex interplay between structural forces and agency. Everyday life is changing more rapidly than ever. People's lifestyles, as well as their selves, are continuously remade and reshaped in new and novel ways. In a period of 'cultural release' (Ziehe 1986), when old traditions lose their hold over people's lives, people increasingly have to take responsibility themselves. This can be very traumatic and difficult. But for people who feel secure and who have the material and mental resources (through upbringing and through belonging to the 'right' cultural networks), contemporary postmodern society offers opportunities for self-expression never offered before.

These changes in everyday life correspond to changes within politics. People with expressivist selves and lifestyles see politics as a domain that is necessarily related to one's personal life. Politics is not something abstract, far removed from everyday life; politics is about self-expression and about immediate action (self-expression obviously does not stand in opposition to collective interests). To this extent it is related to new social movements rather than to traditional political parties. The new social movements make more sense to postmodern people than do traditional parties. In the same way as postmodern people increasingly belong to a number of different networks in everyday life, they also increasingly belong to a number of political groupings, continuously moving between, and in and out of, them. This, in turn, creates an intriguing situation for the state to deal with, as we will discuss.

This book draws on many different sources and disciplines. It also addresses a number of different issues. That may make the book hard to read on occasion. However, as we discuss in the Postscript, there really is no other way to proceed in order to make analyses of this kind meaningful. The book is aimed at people coming from, for instance, political science, political theory, social theory and cultural studies. Some readers may be more interested in some of our analyses, and other readers in other analyses. However, we hope that most readers will read the book in a linear fashion. There are things that we wish to articulate in as clear a manner as possible. In this respect, the book's narrative and objective is probably more modern than postmodern. Which, of course, suggests both the intricate and complex relationship between the two notions *and* the – possibly necessary – ambivalent position we as writers hold towards them.

1

The Languages of Postmodernism

Language, since the writings of Wittgenstein and Foucault, has come to be seen as a political phenomenon. From Wittgenstein we learn that words mean what the users negotiate them to mean in the everyday business of exchange. Users struggle not only to understand others, but to deploy their own meanings in usage. Meaning, in addition, is relative to and contingent upon a system of language generally associated with a particular form of life, such as cookery or politics. From Foucault we learn that terms and discourses are never neutral but are tied to particular epistemes, practices and regimes. They are never of universal application but always contingent, tied to particular times, sites, situations and conflicts.

From Gallie (1955–6/1962) and Connolly (1983) we learn that many terms, and especially political terms, are essentially contested. This means they are internally complex; their usages are various and open for debate. Prescriptive outcomes and hence power are entailed in the acceptance of a usage, and eternal and violent debates often take place over their meaning. Connolly, summarizing the findings of deconstructionists such as Foucault, concluded that every act of speaking or defining, every classification and categorization, is 'actually composed of an arbitrary constellation of elements held together by powers and metaphors which are not inherently rational' (1983: 231).

The languages of postmodernism, we argue, conform to this understanding of the central and power-situated nature of language. The languages are all internally complex, open, appraisive and fought over. The exercise below runs the risks envisioned by Foucault of being a discursive practice, and of imposing participation in the knowledge/power complex; of simply bidding for the reader's accession, and hence ensuring future subjugation. But it is important to recognize that not only is postmodernism important for the understanding and direction of politics; its language and vocabulary are implicated and implicit in today's political discourses and practices. Analysing postmodernism is itself a political activity, a struggle for power as well as comprehension.

Genealogy, or the retrospective understanding and disordering of the past by the recovery of disqualified usages, classifications and discursive practices, is beyond the scope of this chapter. But genealogies of a sort have arisen in recent literature and can provide a useful vehicle for both classification and critical reflection. One recent study in particular is both well researched and useful, that by Margaret Rose (1991), and it will be used as the core of our own analysis.

Rose's aim is a distinctly modern one: 'to bring clarity into the discussion of the term' (1991: xi). Clarity, we reflect, may only be purchased at the cost of rationalization and simplification. Rose achieves this by providing 'an historical and analytic overview of the most influential or significant uses of the terms in question and then a critical analysis of the presuppositions and arguments used with them in recent theories and applications' (1991: xi–xii). In Wittgensteinian terms, as the revelation of plural and contextual meanings via a language game, the exercise is helpful, but Foucauldians may find fault with the aim of bringing clarity to a field where conflict and power struggles reign supreme. Our aim here is initially to exemplify differences and distinctions; to reveal the diversity and contested and ironic nature of the languages and discourses. Only then do we elaborate a specific glossary and usage to guide the reader of this book.

The Modern and the Postmodern

Complex terms with multiple usages attract conflation and confusion. Much writing on postmodern politics to date has focused on these matters. The complexities of postmodernism are furthermore multiplied as we toy with both 'post' and with postmodern's binary opposite, the 'modern'. 'Post' is sometimes used to mean a 'break from' or as a 'continuation of its modern components, or as an amalgamation, or dialectic, of break and continuation' (Rose 1991: 2). It also refers to 'opposition to', 'difference to and from', and 'a response to'. In short, the 'post' in postmodern is not definitive and it is up to writers to clarify their particular usage and not to conflate different meanings. If irony is the characteristic feature of a postmodern treatment of language, as Rorty (1989) and Lemert (1992) argue, then we should note the ironic lessons of 'post' used to mean a system of communication via letters; the mail; items sent in the communication system; a significant location for people; an upright support. Used in conjunction with other terms, 'post' generally refers to 'after' and 'opposed to', as with

8

'post-impressionism', 'post-diluvial', 'postgraduate' and 'postnatal'.

The 'modern' in postmodern is equally ambiguous, elusive and promiscuous (Connolly 1988: 1–60). It may refer to a particular epoch or period in history (Toynbee); the spirit of that age (Mill); a type of thought (Barry); a type of experience (Mannheim); a social category (Weber); a type of political regime (Poggi); a view of the world (Mills); a cultural phenomenon (Featherstone); a style, for example the mod (Hebdige); a type of art, aesthetic medium or style of architecture (Jencks). Irony suggests attention to the original Latin term *modo* and the popular reference to the recent or of today; the popular and the bad in the popular; the commonplace; a style of print face; a term of abuse; a term of approval. Conjoined to 'pre', it generally means before, prior or previous to an epoch or period; less sophisticated; old-fashioned; dated; not worth bothering with. While all may be used in relation to politics, it is most common for the modern to refer to a period variously dated from after the fourteenth century in the West, with its concurrent social, governmental and economic organization, unique logic, thought and culture.

Four terms related to modern also need to be elaborated upon as their binary opposites feature centrally in the languages and discourses of postmodernism, namely modernity, modernize, modernization and modernism. *Modernity* is commonly used to refer to the way of life and state of mind of those experiencing the modern period. It refers to the experience of the economic, social, political, cultural, aesthetic and intellectual life 'that implies the progressive economic and administrative rationalization and differentiation of the social world (Weber, Tönnies, Simmel); processes which brought into being the modern capitalist-industrial state' (Featherstone 1988: 197–198). Characterization of this mood – this sense of the period – is highly contested, with the Comtean thrill at the prospect of progress measured in wealth, health and well-being at one end of a spectrum and dystopian accounts of alienation, discontinuity and panic in the writings of Dostoevsky at the other. But modernity can also refer to a particular historical phase. In this sense, modernity stands for the modern – as opposed to the traditional – period in history; a period that in turn may be divided into, for instance, early, high and late modernity (Fornäs 1995: 47).

Modernize and *modernization* are related, with the first referring to conformity to processes of adaptation from pre-modern to modern, and the second being the processes themselves. Modernize refers variably to adaptation to the present time and adaptation to the modern time. It has more specific uses in various disciplines and paradigms such as adaptation to the new economy in developmental studies; adaptation to new spelling and grammar in literature; to new needs in social policy; and to new ways of life in sociology and anthropology. We shall try to use the term neutrally. We will use it to refer to the multitude of often conflicting and contradictory processes that characterize a certain age. Generally, however, it is used to describe adaptation in a linear and determined framework as in Bell, Rostow and Eisenstadt. In the social sciences these linear models are often structuralist and economistic, but they can also be tied to military, geographical, social, cultural and intellectual forces. Modernization is used throughout the social sciences as a general category for the multitude of processes which cause, accompany or follow the transformation from the pre-modern to the modern. In political science the dominant usage is to refer to the developments that accompany the transformation to an industrial and mechanized society, namely the growth of new classes, social mobility, growth of welfare states, the triumph of scientific and technical knowledge, mass education and culture, and the emergence of political parties and the modern state. In sociology the unilinear models suggest convergence of all societies on an ideal type composite of America, Germany and Japan, often called industrial (Kumar 1978: 185–240). Modernization we consider to be a contested concept, and the one most prone to conflation and misunderstanding. Our usage will be elaborated in the following chapter.

Modernism is the most value-laden term in our family. It can refer to a contemporary usage or expression; a tendency to adapt to new ways; the new ways and practices themselves; a new formalist literary style of criticism (Kermode); a collective term for the diverse intellectual movements opposing naturalism, realism, positivism, that is, romanticism, symbolism, impressionism, and surrealism, often dated between 1850 and 1950; a theological movement aiming to adapt new critical studies; an example of contemporary usage. This ties to the term 'modernist', a person who has adapted him- or herself to the new order, or who is a member of the movement actively promoting modernisms, the avant-garde. There is a risk, however, in assigning to modernism and modernists too much of an intellectual and high culture emphasis. Instead, we regard modernisms and modernists as movements and people trying to *make sense* of modernity. Thus, surrealism is

11

one type of a modernist movement, but other types may be more oriented to popular culture. The 'mod' movement in Britain in the 1960s is one obvious example, but there are of course many others.

Tracing the Postmodern

Rose's most significant contribution to understanding the postmodern is her unrivalled historical study of its usage. Put alongside Rosenau's brief 'Glossary of Post-Modern Terms' (1992: xi–xiv), we have the basis of map, guide and traveller's phrasebook to the post-modern.

Abridging her history, we can chart the first usage of the postmodern to Federico de Onís in 1934, meaning the anti-modernist current in some Spanish and Latin American poetry between 1905 and 1914, a term repeated by the editors of one anthology of such poetry in 1942 (Rose 1991: 13). Bisecting this date span in 1939 was the introduction of the epochal usage by Arnold Toynbee in 1939 to refer to the triumph of mass society after 1914, and adopted by his editor D. C. Somervell in 1946 (Rose 1991: 9). Usage to refer to a period was revived in 1959 when C. Wright Mills referred to a 'Fourth Epoch' in his classic text *The Sociological Imagination* (1959). A third usage, reminiscent of the later popularizing work of Jencks and referring to an intellectual realist reaction to modernist abstract aesthetics and architectural styles, was coined concurrently by Bernard Smith (1945) and Joseph Hudnut (1945; cf. Rose 1991: 14,18). This has developed into the widest usage outside of the social sciences in the fields of literary analysis and criticism.

Rose's study, ambitious and far-reaching as it is, does

not of course cover every possible usage of the term. A fourth recently recovered philosophic usage refers to the 'nihilism' of twentieth-century Western culture, symbolized in the work of Friedrich Nietzsche (Cahoone 1996; Pannwitz 1917). In addition, Rose misses the theologian Bernard Iddings Bell, who in 1939 used the term in a way reminiscent of Bellah to refer to the failure of secularism to supply an acceptable replacement for religion. A sixth usage that has come to dominate in the social sciences developed in the 1970s, namely the usage to refer to the discoveries of post-structuralist philosophers in France and anti-foundationalists in America, the discoveries that language, knowledge, morality and aesthetics had no absolute foundations and that truth and right were relative and contingent. This is generally related to Derrida (1982) and Lyotard (1984) in France and to Rorty (1979, 1983, 1989) in America (though the latter eschews the usage and attacks its adherents as 'posties'), but the general picture of fragmentation, pluralism and incommensurability in the canons of knowledge and culture was spelt out earlier in the writings of Ihab Hassan (1971/1982). Finally, in this tradition we have a usage of postmodern that refers to a dystopian understanding of the age, 'a nihilism of meaning' based upon a conception of the dislocation of images and meaning, referent and referred, representation and reality (Baudrillard 1981). Indeed this anti-representational view that we now live in a world of signs unhinged from their deeper significance is seen as one of the most central and repeated claims in post-modern usage. Endless consumption, the manufacture of images and simulations has, according to Baudrillard, altered the logic of capitalism forever by making consumption rather than production the chief basis of the social order (Bertens 1995: 146).

Social science has produced several adaptations and some new usages for its own needs in recent decades. One marks a restructuring of Marxist theory and practice. In this usage, amplified by Harvey (1989), Smart (1993) and Cochrane (1998), postmodernism refers to the superstructural aspect of late disorganized capitalism; to the cultural and intellectual dimension of late modernity. Poststructuralist claims are repudiated as changes at the political level in the state, parties, cities and in cultural practices, all can, in the end 'be accounted for by an historical materialist analysis of transformations underway within contemporary capitalism towards more flexible forms of accumulation' (Smart 1993: 23).

Another usage was initiated by and around the journal *Theory, Culture & Society* (Featherstone 1985, 1988) to refer to the processes by which cultural forces such as consumerism produce effects at the social level. This usage builds upon the breakdown of the binaries high and low, and elite culture and popular culture, and it places emphasis on the growth of consumer culture. Yet a third and unique usage of the term builds upon the French post structuralist tradition and refers to the disruptive effect of image production, simulation and consumerism on lifestyle and subcultures such as youth groups and new social movements, and hence on the political system. Here postmodernism is related to 'shifting frameworks of power and resistance' (Squires 1993: 1–3); to 'new politics', 'new values' and the reshaping of politics around issues of identity, difference and lifestyle (Connolly 1991; Gibbins 1989a, 1989b; Gibbins and Reimer 1995; Reimer 1989; Ryan 1988).

14

Finally, emancipatory, participatory and democratic resurgence are themes of a usage of postmodernism when related to politics. Three versions of this usage emerged in the 1980s and 1990s: the feminist postmodernisms of Nicholson (1990), Young (1993) and Heckman (1990); the socialist postmodernisms of Laclau and Mouffe (1985; Mouffe 1988) and Yeatman (1994); and the sexual postmodernisms of Weeks (1995) and Squires (1993).

Making Sense of the Postmodern

How do we make sense of these different usages? There is obviously no way that we may argue for one, 'correct' usage of the term. That was never the objective. What we have wanted to do is to show the contested nature of the discourse surrounding postmodernism. From there on, what we *can* do is to position ourselves within the discourse and outline how we intend to use the relevant terms.

In relation to the terms 'modernization', 'modernity' and 'modernism', Fornäs (1995: 38–39) has argued that these could be related to each other as different modes of the modern. For him, modernization is the process leading to modernity as a state, and modernisms are movements of response to that state. Similarly, we will refer to postmodernity as the current historical phase. By postmodernization we mean the processes that shape and characterize postmodernity. By postmodernism we mean aesthetic, cultural, political and academic attempts to make sense of postmodernity.

The above stated definitions will be elaborated upon in subsequent chapters in this book, and then primarily in relation to politics. Before so doing, it may be useful, however, to discuss the theoretical standing of the post-modern discourse.

Postmodernism is regularly used as a term of derision, indicating a kind of thought that is at best woolly and essentially confused – and at worst misguided and dangerous. This usage is itself pluralistic as the objects of attack are various. But the essence is that postmodernism is lazy thinking; that the denial of absolutes is a surrender from the human search for the true and the right; that the denial of foundations only releases theorists from the burden of proof and finding evidence; and that the defenders of postmodernism mistake change within modernity for a radical break. Those usages are popular in the mass media – especially in arts programmes and cultural fora – as well as in academic circles.

This critique is understandable to a certain degree. First, as we have tried to show, there are many competing versions of postmodernism, and the mere fact that it cannot be easily pinned down makes some people – both within and outside academia – nervous. Second, the quoted belief and fact that many adherents to postmodern political configurations are ex-Marxists and socialists, disillusioned feminists or members of professions threatened by or reorganized in post-Fordist restructurings of society reinforces their opponents' beliefs that postmodernists are either naive, utopian dreamers or cynics. However, there is a big difference between being a dreamer and a cynic. And furthermore, these two positions may be reformulated more neutrally to designate two major types of postmodernists. Rosenau (1992: 22–23, 144–155) labels these two groupings 'affirmatives' and 'sceptics'.

This last binary is one useful way to understand the

difference between, on the one side, the essentially critical and deconstructive efforts of the poststructuralists and the post-Marxists and, on the other, the more affirmative beliefs in the capacity of individuals and groups to emancipate and express themselves, in the work of those focusing on new politics, identity, difference and the consumer society.

Sceptics are political agnostics who advocate withdrawal, whereas affirmatives are optimists who advocate participation. The former seek solace in the non-political, whereas affirmatives advocate participation in new movements and politics. Sceptics consider absolute assertions of truth and right, and of practices premised upon them, to be meaningless and dangerous. For them, nihilism, uncertainty and relativity are the only facts of life and politics. They are especially denunciatory about assertions of the unity and identity of subjects and selves. Affirmatives are more confident about subjects and the self. They seek the reflexive construction of new types of subjects and new identities. For them, poststructuralism, deconstruction and postmodernism make spaces where possibilities for experiments in living and new political formations thrive.

The following analyses will be carried out from the perspective of the affirmative postmodernist. We will try to show what politics 'means' in an age of postmodernity, taking into account structural forces as well as human agency, without forgetting the constraints put, and the possibilities offered, by language in expressing this meaningfully.

Taking an affirmative rather than a sceptical stand may in one sense be regarded as an a priori move; a move based in the belief in human agency. But it is not a stand taken blindly, against evidence to the contrary. We will naturally have to argue for our views. In so doing, we will use the language and theories associated with the analysts of new times, with new politics and with the emancipatory activities of new cultural movements. While we accept the standpoints of others, we deny they have a monopoly on truth and will defend our case for a postmodernism without structural determination; a postmodernism which places high explanatory value on cultural change, and which is politically affirmative.

2

Postmodernization

We argued in Chapter 1 that postmodernization stands for the processes that shape postmodernity. In this chapter we will outline in detail the character of these forces. This is not an easy task, however. The concept of postmodernization as such has very seldom been used. The main exception is Crook et al.'s *Postmodernization* (1992). Otherwise the concept is basically non-existent within contemporary social analysis. According to the *Social Sciences and the Arts & Humanities Citation Index*, between 1992 and 1997 only four articles or reviews were published with 'postmodernization' in the title. As a comparison, during the same period more than 500 articles or reviews had 'modernization' in their titles, and more than 800 had 'postmodernism' in their titles. We will therefore initially make use of the discussions centred on the concept of modernization. But moving into this discourse is something of a minefield.

Using the concept of modernization as a basis for a discussion of postmodernization should be rather unproblematic. At least this would be the case if the concept had been used in a 'neutral' way; if it had been used in order to outline the multitude of often conflicting and contradictory processes that characterize a certain age. However, the problem with the concept of modernization is that the customary way of using the concept has not been that neutral. Quite the opposite. To a much greater degree than the concepts of modernity and modernism, from the 1950s onwards the concept of modernization is tied to a rather unilinear and predetermined way of viewing societal changes. It is tied to an a priori view of seeing such changes as determined by economic development (Eisenstadt 1987; Robertson and Lechner 1985). In this sense, the discourse on post-industrialization, with its emphasis on linear transformations, is in many ways a more logical successor to the discourse on modernization than is the discourse on postmodernization (cf. Bell 1973).

The 'traditional' modernization perspective is still very lively within the social sciences. Analyses using the term 'modernization' are still more often than not focused upon economic processes, whereas this very seldom is the case when it comes to analyses using the term 'modernity'. Thus, in order to use the concept of modernization in a more fruitful manner, it is necessary first to strip it of its economistic connotations. The processes in modernity, as well as the processes in postmodernity, can never be reduced to developments within the economy. It may very well be that at certain points in time and in certain contexts, economic factors are prime movers. This may even be the case more often than not. However, whether this is the case is an empirical matter, a matter for the analysis to show, not something to be decided upon a priori. The starting point for the analysis must be to analyse economic factors together with other relevant factors. That is a way of proceeding that is typical of recent analyses of modernity and postmodernity (analyses that, furthermore, increasingly are carried out with the use of the concept of modernization, if not postmodernization, as in Beck et al.'s [1994] book *Reflexive Modernization*). It is in a sense *the* common reference point for analyses of modernity and postmodernity within critical theory (Habermas 1990), contemporary social theory (Giddens 1990, 1991) and cultural studies (Hall and Gieben 1992), and it is within this line of thinking that we position ourselves.

Stuart Hall makes a distinction between political, economic, social and cultural processes, and he argues that these together have given modern societies a distinctive shape and form. Modern societies have become what he calls *social formations*, 'societies with a definite structure and a well-defined set of social relations' (1992: 7). In the words of Habermas:

> The concept of modernization refers to a bundle of processes that are cumulative and mutually reinforcing; to the formation of capital and the mobilization of resources; to the development of the forces of production and the increase in the productivity of labour; to the establishment of centralized political power and the formation of national identities; to the proliferation of rights of political participation, of urban forms of life, and of formal schooling; to the secularization of values and norms; and so on. (1990: 2)

The main processes of modernization, as seen in Habermas's description, include the forces of capitalism, industrialization, secularization, urbanization and nationalization. In this version, modernity is capitalist, it is based on nation states, it is highly secularized and it is urban. To this we may add that modernity increasingly has become a mass media-dominated society. On another level, the way modernity has evolved, in the workplace as well as in leisure spheres, is through an increasing *rationalization* of these spheres. This has coincided with an increasing *differentiation*. Work is separated from leisure, and the private from the public.

Processes of Postmodernization

The processes of modernization shaped modernity. Similarly, we argue, the processes of postmodernization shape postmodernity. What, then, do we mean by postmodernization, as opposed to modernization, processes, and what is postmodernity as opposed to modernity?

In our view, it is more reasonable to characterize contemporary Western societies as postmodern than as modern. By this we mean that Western societies during the last decades have changed significantly. This does not mean that there is not a great deal of continuity between the two kinds of societies, or that the differences are as strong as those between traditional and modern societies, but it means that the changes are substantial enough to warrant this distinction.

There are many ways to describe the differences between modernity and postmodernity. For instance, in comparison with modernity, postmodernity has been identified with a move towards disorganized capitalism, with consumerism, with increasing speed and perpetual change, with an emphasis on surfaces and images, with the mass media, with globalization, with unpredictability, with a questioning of reality and even with the end of the social (Crook et al. 1992; Lash and Urry 1994; Lyon 1994; Smart 1993).

It would be difficult to try to fit all of the characteristics presented above into one, logical framework, and that is not our intention. The literature and debate on postmodernity is enormous, and with people coming to the debate from different discourses and for very different reasons, there will quite naturally not be a framework commonly agreed upon.

We will not give a detailed discussion of the different positions taken in this debate; that has been carried out a number of times already (Lyon 1994; Smart 1993). It is important to remember, however, that the views on postmodernity are neither necessarily positive nor negative. Rosenau's (1992) distinction between sceptical and affirmative postmodernists, discussed in the previous chapter, is a useful reminder of this. Postmodernity contains elements that may make a wonderful society, as well as a terrible one. That is not given a priori. It is decided in historically specific settings. This means that the critique raised towards postmodernism and ideas of postmodernity based on postmodernism's inherent nihilism is valid only against one kind of postmodernism. Therborn writes: 'Modernity ends when words like progress, advance, development, emancipation, liberation, growth, accumulation, enlightenment, embetterment, avant-garde, lose their attraction and their function as guides to social action' (1995a: 4). That would be true in relation to a sceptical postmodernist but not in relation to an affirmative one. We will not move further into the sceptical/affirmative debate at this stage. Instead we will highlight a number of characteristics that we see as crucial in the formation of postmodernity; characteristics that, furthermore, are interconnected.

We will focus on the *unpredictability* of contemporary societies. Contemporary societies are becoming increasingly complex and they are changing faster than ever before. This makes it very difficult to know what the end result of different processes will be. Postmodernity is still dominated by capitalism but it is not the same capitalism that dominated modernity. Postmodernity's capitalism is *disorganized* (Lash and Urry 1994).

One reason behind the increasing unpredictability in relation to societal change is that the world is 'shrinking'. *Globalization* processes are increasingly shaping postmodernity. We live in a world in which things happening in one part of the globe can have an enormous impact in another. This is as true for things happening at a stock market as it is for things happening at a nuclear plant. We live today in a common 'risk society' (Beck 1992).

But we also live in a *mass media society*. An increasing part of our everyday life experiences is mediated rather than direct. It is through the mass media that we are aware of what is happening in other parts of the world. Information and communication technologies play an ever more important role in everyday life. With the help of such technologies, including of course the Internet and email, it is becoming possible to uphold personal contacts daily with people living on other continents. Our social spheres are increasingly becoming uncoupled from our physical spheres (Meyrowitz 1985).

Thus, in our view, postmodernity is characterized by *disorganized capitalism*, by *globalization* and by *mediazation*. These are the structures and processes that more than others make contemporary Western societies into postmodern societies. By this we do not mean that postmodernity entails a radical and a complete break with modernity. There are obviously continuities. We still live in societies shaped by class and gender, for instance. However, in our view, the differences are still strong enough to warrant this distinction: the scope, the speed and the number of forces have increased to the extent that, instead of modernity and modernization, we prefer to speak of postmodernity and postmodernization, and the structures and processes that more than others shape contemporary Western societies are the ones stated here. Of these, the first two we will deal with in this chapter. The mass media will be dealt with in the next chapter.

Disorganized Capitalism

One major feature of modernity, in relation to traditional societies, is that things change at an ever-increasing pace. Society becomes ever more complex and the only constant is change itself: 'All that is solid melts into air' (Berman 1982). This is of course true also for postmodernity. It could furthermore be argued that the pace continues to increase. This may be seen, for instance, in changes occurring in the work sector, as well as in changes having to do with lifestyle choices. The increase in pace may in itself not be so novel. However, the faster contemporary societies change, and the more complex they become, the more difficult it becomes to foresee or predict the consequences of different kinds of action. Postmodern society is more *unpredictable* than modern society was.

Lash and Urry (1994) argue that capitalism on its way to postmodernity has gone through three stages. In the first stage, during the nineteenth century, 'liberal capitalism' operated on the level of locality or region. In the second stage, in the twentieth century, 'organized capitalism' operated on the level of the nation. Now, in postmodernity, capitalism has become 'disorganized'. The circulation of goods and capital takes place on an international level. There is an increasing *flow* of both objects (money and commodities) and subjects (labour power) across borders. These subjects and objects travel increasing distances and with increasing speed, making it more and more difficult to synchronize the processes, thereby making the system as such even more disorganized.

Speed and change are important factors in this process. The production process underlying organized capitalism is often called Fordism, namely the production of products on a large scale as cheaply as possible for a large group of consumers. In order to do this, products have to be highly standardized and the planning of products has to be centralized. Fordism obviously derives its name from the assembly-line production pioneered by Henry Ford, but the principles as such are valid not only for the production of cars or even goods in general. They may equally well be utilized within agriculture, within the service sector or within the culture industries.

In postmodernity this process has changed. Today, consumers are increasingly reluctant to accept a lack of choice between alternative products, or between alternative versions of the same product. They want to make choices. Furthermore, with the accelerated pace of everyday life, consumers want products for shorter periods of time. This means that production has to be focused upon short series with a scope for flexibility aimed at a heterogeneous customer group as opposed to long series of standardized products aimed at a homogeneous group of consumers. Within post-Fordism, flexibility is the key word (Harvey 1989; Kumar 1995; Murray 1989).

Furthermore, the balance of production is switching

from traditional material goods to signs. What is increasingly being produced – and consumed – are non-material objects containing primarily aesthetic components (cinema, pop music, etc.). But the sign value in material objects is also increasing. Material objects are becoming aestheticized, both by producers and by consumers. Producers spend lots of money both on advertising and on design, and consumers buy products that send the 'right' signals to other people. The aesthetic and cultural component of a product increasingly determines its value (Lash and Urry 1994: 15).

In relation to the processes of rationalization and differentiation, it could be argued, first, that post-Fordism is as rational as Fordism. The logic of post-Fordism is different from the logic of Fordism, but it is still based on a process of rationalization, of trying to make one's organization as efficient as possible. However, post-Fordism demands more of its practitioners. Decisions have to be made faster and on the basis of less safe knowledge. Consumer behaviour is becoming more and more difficult to predict.

Second, the process of differentiation is becoming more complex. In modernity social life became more and more rational through the separation of different spheres. Work was split from leisure, and from home. New institutions such as schools and hospitals took over responsibilities that earlier belonged to families. In postmodernity this process seems to continue in some areas, but in others, the process seems to be reversing.

On the one hand, post-Fordism indicates that people have different needs; they cannot be treated like one homogeneous group. This means that through the use of different products, and through fashion, people express themselves differently (Kratz and Reimer 1998). There is an increasing differentiation when it comes to people's lifestyles. There is, furthermore, an increasing differentiation on the level of aesthetic and cultural products. The number of genres is increasing. If in modernity it was possible to distinguish between rock and pop, for instance, in postmodernity the boundaries between genres may be found between, for instance, speed metal and heavy metal. A similar argument can of course be made for film or TV genres.

But postmodernity is not only about differentiation. It is also argued that today we are actually witnessing a process of *de-differentiation*, a process in which the typical spheres of modernity are once again losing some of their distinctness (Lash and Urry 1994: 272; cf. Crook et al. 1992). This can be seen in the relationships between work and leisure and between the private and the public: with the help of personal computers and the Internet people are able to work at home. But it is also visible in relation to aesthetic and cultural products. The relationships between reality and fiction, and between news and entertainment, are becoming blurred, and so is the relationship between high culture and popular culture. The question of cultural 'quality' has become more difficult in postmodernity. The whole hierarchical system within which the spheres belong is questioned; there is no principle according to which the system is ordered (cf. Kumar 1995: 101–104).

In this context it is relevant to refer to what Giddens (1991: 17–21) has called the *disembedding*, as opposed to the differentiation, of social institutions. Giddens argues that differentiation only indicates a specialization and separation of functions. It does not capture the most crucial feature of the process, namely the fact that in postmodernity social relations are increasingly 'lifted out' of local contexts; they lose their necessary connection to local place. Instead their roles are replaced and taken over by abstract systems, primarily money and expert systems. Money makes it possible to conduct business transactions without face-to-face encounters, and expert systems (systems consisting of technicians, doctors, therapists, etc.) make it possible to conduct similar kinds of services no matter who is conducting the services. This is one part of the globalization process.

Globalization

As argued above, postmodernity is partly shaped by processes characteristic of modernity. But those forces are not the only ones having a great impact on postmodernity. One other process has become increasingly important in postmodernity: *globalization*.

Globalization can be traced back to at least the early fifteenth century in Europe (Robertson 1992: 58), but has during the twentieth century made an impact in more and more parts of the world – even though the process is by no means complete. It is, however, a process that is gaining increasing academic attention. As Waters argues, 'just as postmodernism was *the* concept of the 1980s, globalization may be *the* concept of the 1990s' (1995: 1). Globalization is currently an important topic within a number of different disciplines, including political science, sociology, anthropology, cultural geography, media studies and cultural studies (cf. Featherstone 1991; Featherstone et al. 1995; King 1991; Mohammadi 1997; Waters 1995).

For Robertson, one of the main globalization

theorists, 'Globalization as a concept refers both to the compression of the world and the intensification of consciousness of the world as a whole' (1992: 8). In other words, Robertson sees globalization as both a macro-process and as the awareness of such a process. It is in many ways an elegant definition, and it has been taken up also by other writers (cf. Waters 1995: 3). However, we prefer to see globalization primarily as a macro-level process, just like mediazation, urbanization, industrialization and post-industrialization. All of these processes no doubt have an impact on everyday life, and people are more or less aware of their existence. However, that does not mean that the processes as such necessarily become micro-level phenomena. In our view, it is more reasonable to treat the phenomena as macro-level phenomena, and to analyse the role they have on micro-level action.

Thus, by globalization we mean those macro-level processes that make the world more interconnected and altogether smaller. The world is shrinking through a process that the cultural geographer David Harvey (1989) calls time–space compression. Due to new communication and information technologies, spatial distances are losing their importance. It is today possible to keep daily contacts with people living on other continents, and through the mass media, the same event may be experienced all over the world. The Internet, as mentioned above, is but the latest example of how the world continues to shrink.

Globalization is not only about technologies, however. The globalization process also involves the rise of transnational corporations, the increase in international trade, increasing levels of immigration and travel. And it most definitely includes increasing interconnectedness in relation to risk and danger. Ecological and military threats can no longer easily be contained to specific areas. We all live in what Ulrich Beck terms a 'risk society' (1992), a common society in which space no longer may protect a nation and its citizens from accidents and disasters happening in other countries or even on other continents.

One of the main questions for globalization research is *political*. It concerns the nation state and its future. It is argued that a number of factors together threaten the traditional role played by the state: a growing number of economic corporations take the form of transnational corporations; the cultural bonds between people from different states tend to become stronger; new social movements such as Greenpeace and Friends of the Earth have a global focus; and, maybe most importantly, states increasingly become members of, and at occasions even give up their sovereignty to, supranational organizations; organizations such as the UN, NATO, the EU and OPEC (McGrew 1992).

Another main question is *economic*. It concerns the relationships between actors involved in economic transactions. The globalization process has led to increasing trade between nations. But this trade is highly structured. It is based on an international division of labour; a division between capital-intensive production in some countries and labour-intensive in others. This division of labour is leading to a widening gap between rich and poor countries (Waters 1995).

Increasingly, however, attention has been focused on *cultural* globalization. Similarly to economic relationships, cultural relationships are unequally structured. A few countries, with the United States as

31

the unquestionable leader, export their cultural products to the rest of the world. As argued by the media researcher Herbert Schiller: 'The worldwide impact of the transnational cultural industries . . . may be as influential as other, more familiar, forms of (US) power; industrial, military, scientific. . . . People everywhere are consumers of (mostly) American images, sounds, ideas, products and services' (1996: 115).

In this view, cultural globalization is really a one-way process of cultural imperialism. American projects are exported around the world, and the world is becoming increasingly homogenized, according to American standards. Different cultures have always influenced each other, but never before has the process been so one-sided, it is argued (Hamelink 1983; Schiller 1976, 1996).

There is no doubt a lot of truth to these statements, at least in the sense that the export and import of mass-mediated culture are in no ways evenly matched between different countries – even though the United States is not by any means the only country exporting media products to other countries; other main exporters include India, Egypt, Mexico and Brazil (Sreberny-Mohammadi 1996).

However, some problems exist with the above statements. First of all, they give a romanticized picture of what, for instance, third world cultures looked like before the United States imposed its culture on them. Most third world cultures were not authentic in the sense that they were untainted by foreign influences. Rather, the cultures had already, pre-United States, been shaped through often brutal conflicts; conflicts in which traditional customs had been destroyed (cf. Thompson 1995: 169–170).

Second, it is taken for granted that cultural homogenization is necessarily a bad thing. But, as John Tomlinson (1991: 110) has argued, there are a number of cultural practices that most people probably would like to find in action all over the world; practices such as democratic processes, health care, food hygiene and liberal cultural attitudes toward tolerance and compassion.

Third, it is important to distinguish between the export of, for instance, American television programmes to other countries and the actual outcome of the viewing of these programmes. The viewing of a TV programme is always taking place in a specific cultural context and the meaning of such viewing cannot be read straight off the programme. Different people interpret similar programmes in different ways depending upon, among other things, cultural background. We will return to this matter in more detail in the next chapter.

And fourth, an exclusive focus on homogenization processes may actually give a questionable picture of contemporary globalization forces. Robertson argues: 'It is not a question of *either* homogenization or heterogenization, but rather of the ways in which both of these tendencies have become features of life across much of the late-twentieth-century world' (1995: 27).

Robertson's point is that the processes in contemporary disorganized societies are quite complex. They cannot be reduced to a single process of homogenization. Elaborating on this statement, Appadurai (1990) distinguishes between five different dimensions of global cultural flow that the global processes influence: ethnoscapes (the flow of tourists, immigrants, guestworkers), technoscapes (the flow of technology between countries), finanscapes (the flow of money), ideoscapes (the flow of ideologies) and mediascapes (the flow of media images).

According to Appadurai, these different scapes all have their own internal logic and they are subject to different kinds of constraints. This means that the relationship between them is deeply disjunctive and utterly unpredictable. The ways that a specific country is affected by the global economy may have very little to do with the flow of technology, or with the images presented through global media channels to that country. The disjunction between these flows is furthermore increasing. Appadurai writes: 'the sheer speed, scale and volume of each of these flows is now so great that the disjunctures have become central to the politics of a global culture' (1990: 301). It is in line with this increasing disjuncture that the notion of straightforward cultural homogenization becomes questionable.

Postmodernization and Ambivalence

In this chapter we have discussed the macro-level processes that shape contemporary Western societies. We have done this by using the language of modernization and postmodernization. In concluding this chapter, there are some aspects of our discussion that need to be highlighted.

First, in using the concepts of modernization and postmodernization, it was necessary to make clear that we use these in what could be called a 'contemporary' way. That is, our perspective on the processes is one opposed to simple base–superstructure distinctions, and to economic determinism. As Habermas (1990) argues, the evolution of modernity is the result of the interplay between a number of different processes; an interplay that is highly complex. Sometimes the different processes support each other, sometimes they don't. Sometimes economic factors are primary, sometimes they are not. It is in this context that Bauman (1991) refers to the processes characteristic of modernity as highly ambivalent. It does not mean that the processes are arbitrary, but it means that the outcome of the articulations between the processes are always historically and culturally specific. We agree with the above-described picture of modernity but we would like to add that the characteristic is even more relevant for postmodernity. Crook et al. write: 'the shock of postmodernization is that directionality is totally unclear: the only certainty is continuing uncertainty' (1992: 3).

Second, in this context, we focused primarily on the forces of globalization. These have been important in many ways. The cultural flows, as discussed by Appadurai and others, transgress national borders and create new relationships between the local and the global. They have also given rise to a rethinking of the role of the nation state as the 'natural' unit for the sense of cultural belonging. As Giddens (1991: 32) argues, self and society are for the first time ever interrelated in a global milieu. The processes of modernity created 'imagined communities' of the size of the nation state (Anderson 1991). The processes of postmodernity may alter the size of those communities.

The forces of globalization, furthermore, have entailed an important rethinking of what modernity as such is all about; it has led Westerners to relativize the commonly held ideas of modernity as having one particular 'look'. There are many routes to modernity, not all of them Western (Therborn 1995b). And if we are to focus upon postmodern cities, maybe our attention should be directed towards Rio and Calcutta, not New York and Los Angeles. These cities were multi-cultural, disorganized and schizophrenic decades earlier (King 1995).

Finally, it should have become apparent in reading this chapter that when discussing the forces of post-modernization, we did not draw out the implications of these forces in any detail. We did not state what effects these processes have had on people in contemporary Western societies. There is a perfectly simple reason for this. Macro-level processes do not work that way on people. We cannot say anything meaningful about the role of these processes until we relate them to micro-level processes; until we relate them to how people in concrete, cultural contexts act and react on these processes. That will be the objective of the following chapters.

3
Mass Media, Postmodernity and Everyday Life

We live today in a mass media-saturated environment. The mass media are all around us, from morning till night. We wake up to a clock radio, we read the morning newspaper while eating breakfast, we listen to the radio at work, and we watch television when we come home in the evenings. What has all this meant for our everyday lives? According to some postmodern commentators, the changes have been profound. The lines between reality and illusion have become blurred, it is argued. We live in hyper-reality; in a world where images seem more real than reality itself.

We will treat this question seriously, but we will argue that the changes have not been that far-reaching. Our everyday life environments *have* changed and we do spend an increasing part of our days with the mass media. But the media are still used in concrete, local places, people integrate media use with other everyday life practices, and most people do still have a grip on reality.

In this chapter, we will discuss how people use the media and we will analyse the different roles that the mass media play in postmodernity. We will discuss, furthermore, how mediated communication and interpersonal communication are combined in everyday life. Finally, we will discuss whether we actually live in hyperreality.

Mediazation

In the previous chapter we discussed the macro-processes of postmodernity. We argued that, with the exception of globalization, all of the processes had their origins in modernity. This, of course, is also the case for the mediazation process. The development of the mass media was an integral factor in the formation of modernity – even though, suprisingly enough, the media are often absent in analyses of modernity. In most analyses, the media are in many ways taken for granted as important sources in the makings of modernity, but they are not analysed in any detail. This is the case with Giddens (1990, 1991), for instance. But there are, of course, examples of writings combining a modernity perspective with an interest in the media. John B. Thompson's *The Media and Modernity* (1995) is the standard work of how media have shaped modernity. Other examples of modernity analyses highlighting the media include Habermas's (1962/1989) study of the transformations of the public sphere and Benedict Anderson's (1991) study of the role newspapers played in shaping 'imagined communities'. Within media studies as such, the modernity perspective is surprisingly rare. Recently, however, the perspective has been utilized in relation to new media technologies, for instance in the works of Silverstone (1994) and Moores (1995, 1996).

We will not deal with the media and modernity as such here. Our focus is on postmodernity. What is relevant in this context is that, of all the processes that characterized modernity, the mediazation process is the one that more than any other continues to affect and change social life to even greater extents. That is, not only does the process continue to matter – so do many of the other processes – but it is the continuous evolution of the mediazation process that sets it apart from the other processes. It becomes more and more important at the same time as it changes in ways that are difficult to foresee.

There are six aspects of the mediazation process in postmodernity that we would like to highlight. First, the media culture is increasingly changing from a print culture to an *electronic culture*. The roles played by electronic and print media differ between cultures, of course. In Europe, newspapers are read regularly by a majority of the population, whereas in the United States this is not the case. However, on the whole, print media, although by no means becoming obsolete, are more restricted to certain groups of a society than are electronic media. This is due to the accessibility of electronic media. These media are, of course, not more 'real' than print media, but they are more reminiscent of reality. Television, especially, looks like reality; it is the one medium whose codes basically everyone can understand, even children (cf. Meyrowitz 1985).

Second, the media are increasingly involved in *transnational processes*. Historically, the media assisted in creating nation states as we have come to know them. Through newspapers, people in different parts of a country could feel that they belonged to the same community, even though they would never meet (Anderson 1991). Today, the media do not only portray the national culture. Two important changes have occurred. First, many countries now import a large proportion of their television output. The import is cheap, and it attracts large audiences. And second, satellite broadcasting has meant that people can watch other programmes than the ones offered by their national broadcasting companies.

The distribution of programmes between countries is extremely uneven. Some countries export programmes and other countries import. The United States is by far the greatest exporter, but also other countries play dominating roles in different parts of the world. The programmes available via satellite are to a certain degree the same ones otherwise offered as exports, and in that sense they contribute to an uneven distribution. However, satellite broadcasting has also meant that people living outside their own countries are able to keep in contact with their native culture. Through a process of 'reterritorialization' (García Canclini 1995) it is possible for people who for different reasons have had to leave their home countries to create their specific local version of a distant culture. With the help of mass media products and modern communication technology, Turks are able to maintain contact with Turkish culture while living in Germany, Pakistanis can do so in Britain, and Vietnamese immigrants can uphold a local version of Vietnamese culture in California (Lull 1995: ch. 5).

Third, the media are becoming *increasingly commercialized and deregulated*. Profit has always been an important motive for involvement with the media, and many media businesses have started solely for that reason. However, there have also been ideological and cultural reasons behind media enterprises. In postmodernity, the commercial angle is stronger than ever before. This could be seen in the always commercially dominated American media system but also increasingly in the historically much less commercially dominated Western European media systems. Here, satellite broadcasting has weakened the public service systems and deregulation is on the agenda in many countries.

Fourth, media ownership is increasingly being *concentrated* in a small number of corporations. These corporations are primarily American, Japanese or, increasingly, transnational. A key characteristic of the corporations is that they aim for both vertical and horizontal integration. On the one hand, the corporations try to become involved in all aspects of production and distribution (vertical integration); they produce CDs as well as CD players, and they both produce motion pictures and own the cinemas where the pictures are shown. On the other hand, the corporations try to diversify by moving into related areas within the leisure industry. In both instances, the result is that corporations merge, and become yet larger and more dominant (cf. Burnett 1996; Sreberny-Mohammadi 1996).

Fifth, *new technologies* change the mediazation process. We have already mentioned satellite television, but the Internet, too, exemplifies the constant change to which the media environment is subject. Through the Internet, people can communicate across borders and they can gain information on basically anything without having to deal with the kinds of gate-keepers that control traditional media. At this stage, it is impossible to forecast where this will lead.

And finally, a key characteristic of the mediazation process in postmodernity is the increasing mass media *intertextuality*. Mass media content, and especially television content, is becoming increasingly self-referential. New programmes are based on, and demand of viewers a knowledge of, old programmes. Television is increasingly concerned with itself, and things happening outside the media become less and less important (Fiske 1987).

The Mass Media in Everyday Life

No one can seriously question that the mass media have drastically changed people's everyday lives. A simple indicator of this fact is the amount of time that people spend with the mass media every day. The mass media have without question taken time away from other social practices. But what does this *mean*? How should we interpret the fact that we spend so much time with the mass media, and what are the consequences of this?

For a long period, starting around the 1920s, this question was raised primarily through a media effects perspective. What do the media do to us? Initially, the answer to this question seemed intuitively simple: a lot. This could be deduced simply by looking at the popularity of the cinema and by looking at the importance of propaganda during the two world wars. The mass media seemed to have immediate effects on mass audiences.

This view of simple, short-term effects on large audiences was later questioned. Systematic analyses of media effects made it clear that matters were more complicated. It became clear that if there were media effects, then these were not simple, linear ones, affecting all people in identical ways. Instead, it was necessary to take into account people's different competences as well as their reasons for using the media. For a while, in relation to interpersonal communication, the mass media seemed to be practically powerless.

The introduction of television initiated a new stage in media effects research. Now the mass media once again seemed to be more powerful, although not as all-powerful as once thought. There was, furthermore, a change in focus: from short-term, intended effects on primarily behaviour, to long-term, arguably unintended effects on primarily values and world views.

The picture presented above of the evolution of media effects research is the commonly accepted one (McQuail 1994). Research is today more concerned with long- than with short-term effects, and the views on media effects are more nuanced: the mass media are neither powerless nor all-powerful. However, beyond an agreement on those points, not much is settled within media effects research. There is no consensus whatsoever on how powerful the media are, and under what circumstances. As Livingstone in a recent review of the field states it: 'Despite the volume of research, the debate about media effects . . . remains unresolved' (1996: 306; cf. Reimer 1998).

In one way this situation may seem strange, given the amount of work and money put into the field. On the other hand, trying to give a general answer to the question of media effects may in itself be futile. The field is divided into subfields dealing with different aspects of media effects, such as cultivation analysis, agenda research and spiral of silence research, and maybe it would be more reasonable just to treat these subfields separately (Bryant and Zillman 1994).

However, there may be a more serious problem with

media effects research, and that has to do with the general model on which research is based, a model starting with a transmitter sending a message through a channel to a number of receivers and where the object of research is to trace how accurately the receivers receive the message. It is a model based on a very passive view of human action, and it does not take into account the fact that people in everyday lives do not sit around waiting for separate messages to receive, but rather live in an environment in which they constantly can choose between different messages within their social context and where they decide to receive and make meaning out of some, while they reject others. This may be seen as a distinction between a transmission and a ritual model of communication (Carey 1989).

The kind of critique outlined above has led to alternative perspectives on the role of the media, perspectives that take the audience rather than the media as the point of departure; perspectives that ask the question 'What do we do with the media?' rather than 'What do the media do to us?'

The social science version of this perspective is called 'uses and gratifications' research. It starts with the needs of the audience and analyses how people use the media in order to fulfil those needs. Normally analyses are carried out with the help of large-scale surveys and the interest is in obtaining generalizable knowledge of audience behaviour (Blumler and Katz 1974; Rosengren et al. 1985).

The uses and gratifications perspective on mass media use has a number of weaknesses. First, it has an individualistic bias; it treats people as rational individuals rather than as social beings. Second, it does not pay any particular attention to the media output itself (to the actual 'texts' that people consume). And third, by working with surveys, the perspective is not very useful when it comes to finding out what people actually get out of media use (Reimer 1994).

These types of criticisms have lately been raised particularly by people coming from the humanities. First, studies have been carried out with the explicit focus of trying to understand precisely what different people can get out of similar texts. So-called 'reception analysis' consists of long interviews with a smaller number of people where the focus is on the different kinds of interpretations that people may make of particular texts. Many of the earlier studies within this tradition were carried out by feminist media researchers on typical female genres: romance books and soap operas, particularly. The reason behind doing this research was an interest among feminists as to why these genres have been so popular among housewives. The genres as such were also meaningful to analyse since they are relatively 'open' in character. They are possible to interpret differently since they have many different lead characters with which it is possible to identify and, in the case of soaps, they never finish, making it possible to go on thinking about them (Ang 1985; Liebes and Katz 1990; Radway 1984).

Reception analysis thus treat *texts*, and people's interpretations of them, seriously. Another line of research within humanistic media research has instead concentrated on *contexts*. Within 'mass media ethnography' the focus is on the concrete social and cultural contexts within which mass media use is taking place. Instead of focusing on a concrete text, attention is directed to the role that the mass media play in everyday life in relation to other social and cultural practices, as well as to the way other practices, and other people, play a part in how media are used. This line of research is based both on interviews and on participant observation in the environments where people normally use the media, that is, in their homes (Andersson and Jansson 1997; Lull 1990; Moores 1996; Morley 1986).

Taken together, these two lines of research have shown that mass media use is a much more complex and varied activity than it has been allowed to be within both media effects research and the Uses and Gratifications tradition. Different people get different things out of watching *Dallas*, for instance (Ang 1985). Still, it must be acknowledged that, just as with media effects research, it is very difficult to summarize what reception analysis and mass media ethnography have taught us about the roles of the media in everyday life – albeit for somewhat different reasons.

The problem with reception analysis and media ethnography in this respect is intimately related to their actual ways of proceeding. That is, both perspectives are *micro*-perspectives; they deal with small groups of people and they do so in semi-structured ways. And this constitutes both the strengths and weaknesses of the work. The analyses have given us tremendous detailed knowledge of how different texts are interpreted, of how the same texts may be interpreted differently, of how the workings within a concrete household determine the uses of the media, and of the role that media use plays within the household. Those are the strengths. But most of this knowledge is of a very particular kind. It is very difficult to make systematic comparisons of the studies carried out. This is not a critique of the problems of making generalizable knowledge on the basis of long interviews and participant observation. Rather, the social and cultural contexts within which the media are used are in turn positioned within larger macro-structures that thus far have not been treated seriously enough by these traditions. That is, people do not happen to find themselves in a particular micro-context in a random manner. Due to social and cultural background, some people are more likely to wind up within some micro-contexts than others are, and if human action within particular micro-contexts is to be understood properly, then it is necessary to take into account not only the micro-contexts in themselves but also their surrounding macro-structures. This is a kind of research that still remains to be carried out (Reimer 1997). We will return to this matter in the final section of this chapter.

The Roles of the Mass Media

In the picture of contemporary audience research presented above, we argued that the micro–macro link still is a problematic one. But even with that limitation, it is, of course, possible to make some kind of sense of the roles that the media play in everyday life. We would like to distinguish between four major roles.

First, the media assist in the process of *identity construction*. The media function as a cultural forum. It is increasingly through the media that people get impulses about whom they want to be or whom they want to become. These media impulses are quite contradictory. The media do not tell anyone with an authoritative voice that this is the way he or she should behave. Rather, they constantly tell us different things and it is up to us to choose between these messages.

Out of the complex and varied media output, people turn to the kind of messages that seem *relevant* to them; relevant in their normal, day-to-day situation. It should be pointed out that of the media output, aesthetic and cultural products are especially important for the process of identity construction. It is when consuming such products that it becomes possible for people to leave their normal lives for a while and cross a threshold to something else; in the company of a good book or in the darkness of the cinema it becomes possible to experiment with one's identity and to think through whom one wants to become. Aesthetic and cultural experience thus afford special possibilities for self-reflection (Newcomb and Hirsch 1987).

Second, the media assist in the process of *sense-making*. In a world that is becoming increasingly complex, and where events far away are becoming increasingly important, the more we have to rely on the media in order to make sense of the world. They set the agenda for what we think about (Dearing and Rogers 1996). It is important to emphasize that in this process, both factual and fictional media output are involved. That is, people gain information about the world not only from hard news in the local newspaper or from the evening news on television, but also from soap operas on television or from a thriller in the cinema. The question of whether the world as it is presented in different media and in different genres is more or less accurate is here of less importance. The important point is that people pick out those bits and pieces that make sense to them and from these construct a more or less coherent world view; one that thus will differ from those of other groups.

Third, the media, of course, also give people *pleasure*.

There is a pleasurable aspect involved in much of people's uses of the media. It is immediate, in the sense that it may be pleasurable to watch a specific TV programme or to read a particular book, but there is also a delayed pleasure in the sense that media use gives people things to talk about on other occasions. The pleasure of the media does not stop at the point of consumption. It is important to note that there is no necessary connection between pleasure and entertainment genres. Fiction is relevant for many people's world views, as discussed above. Similarly, for many people reading about hard news in the local newspaper could be as pleasurable for them as the watching of a comedy on television could be for others.

Fourth, the media also assist in the *structuring of everyday life*. Everyday life is based on routines, and the media are used in order to routinize life. People read the morning paper at breakfast, listen to the radio in the car on the way to work and watch the evening news on television every night. And if the paper does not appear in the morning, it may be the loss of something to do while eating (the loss of the routine) that is more problematic than not being able to read the paper in itself (cf. Bausinger 1984).

One important role that the media play in the structuring of everyday life is that they bind together people's different public and private arenas. Television is watched at home but the programmes are discussed in the workplace. A song heard on the car radio is reviewed in the daily paper. The mass media are present in basically every arena that people move between and they constitute objects of discussion when crossing the borders between the arenas. But the media can also change these arenas. Some arenas are private, and some are public, but with the help of the media, private arenas can be made more public and vice versa. Through the Internet, a person's living room can be connected to the other parts of the world. Similarly, through the use of a Walkman on a bus, a public arena can be made more private (Reimer 1995).

An Age of Hyperreality?

In postmodernity the mass media have grown in importance, and so have information and communication technologies generally. This has led a number of postmodern commentators, Baudrillard most notably, to argue that we live in an age of hyperreality. By this, Baudrillard means that computerization, communication technology and the media together frame human experience by producing images and models of reality that are increasingly supplanting reality itself as the guage of what reality 'is'. How do we know what is real? We watch television and we read newspapers and books, and the models of reality presented in these media are the ones we use to gain an impression of reality. We live in hyperreality, a world in which the distinction between reality and the models of reality has become blurred, and in which the models produce, or at least define, reality (Baudrillard 1983; cf. Best and Kellner 1991).

How reasonable is this description of postmodernity, and of people's visions of reality? A problem with it is that it takes a surrounding culture that obviously has changed as an indication that people have also changed in a similar manner. That is, if the culture has to a certain extent become postmodern, then people have also become postmodern. But that does not follow. It is the same kind of mistake made by effects researchers who claim that by looking at a content of a film, it is possible to deduce its effects on an audience.

Baudrillard is extremely fascinated by the United States, by its mass media environment, by Disneyland (1988). For him, a French intellectual, these environments seem unreal. But for most Americans they are perfectly 'natural', not natural in the sense of being nature-given and necessary, but in the sense of having become naturalized. They have been a part of one's daily environment for such a long time that it would feel 'unnatural' if they were not there. This is basically the way most social phenomena find their way into everyday life (cf. Schütz and Luckmann 1973).

For people growing up today, it seems perfectly 'natural' to spend a large proportion of one's daily life with the mass media. Yet we don't have to go that far back in time in order to find a completely different situation. The mass media have, of course, played an important role in society ever since the invention of printing. But the introduction of electronic media unquestionably meant a qualitative change in the way that the media shape everyday life. Through the introduction of first radio and later television, the mass media have captured both time and space in everyday life: space in the sense that the media occupy concrete physical spaces in the homes; and time in the sense that people spend their time in their homes listening to the radio or watching television (Johnson 1981; Moores 1988).

A naturalization process means that people in daily life take phenomena for granted; the phenomena become parts of the daily environment and therefore do not normally warrant any special reflection. They are just there. But this does not mean, as Baudrillard would argue, that people have lost their critical distance to them. As shown in reception analyses, when asked, most people are able to discuss and reflect over why they use the media the way they do. Very few adults are unable to distinguish between an actor and the part he or she is playing.

Thus, the ideas of hyperreality are, as we see it, exaggerated. This does not mean that the media are 'innocent' when it comes to social change or to people's visions of reality. We would even argue that the role of the media is increasing in importance. But instead of talking in sweeping terms of hyperreality and simulacra, it is more meaningful to focus upon more concrete mediazation processes and on their consequences for human action.

We argued in the previous section that the roles the media play are tied to people's constructions both of themselves and of their surrounding societies. They assist in both identity construction and sense-making processes. Furthermore, we argued that people use those parts of the media output that seem relevant, and they use them in a way that makes sense to them.

In postmodernity, as we argued initially in this chapter, the mass media output has grown tremendously. This means that the possibilities are greater than ever before to use the media in highly specific, personal ways. If you want to watch high culture on television, this is now much easier. And if you only want to watch sports, you can do that. In one way, this may be interpreted as part of an individualization process, in which people increasingly choose the life they want to live, regardless of tradition. However, one should be careful when interpreting this process. Of course it is true that people make personal choices in regard to media use, and use the media in ways that make sense to them. But it is important to remember that media use, just like other kinds of social and cultural practices, is to a great extent determined by habits and competences, and by social and cultural background. Thus, unless you grow up in a home in which it seems 'natural' to read high culture books, you may not pick up that habit later in life. High culture does not seem relevant under those circumstances.

This means that the greater media output, and the greater possibilities for people to choose different kinds of media output, may lead not only to an increasing individualization but also to an increasing *polarization*; to increasing differences between different groups of people. Today more than ever before we can use the media for our own purposes. We can use them in order to express ourselves. This is the positive aspect of the mediazation process. But at the same time, with greater differences in people's use of the media there will come a corresponding divergence in the construction of people's individual world views. Different groups of people turn to different parts of the media output and construct different versions of the world, making it increasingly difficult to communicate in meaningful ways. A common public sphere – a sphere in which everyone participates – may become increasingly difficult to uphold. That is the more negative aspect of the mediazation process. It is necessary to keep both of these aspects in mind simultaneously.

4

The Postmodern Self

Postmodernization as a process acts upon the self and the groups to which selves belong. Here we explore the effects of postmodernization and the self's range of responses, before going on to analyse the behavioural response in lifestyle, politics, the state and the international order. We eschew any idea of causality and of linear development in this process, preferring this sequence of presentation only because the resulting story may be more coherent to readers attuned to modern social science narratives. The self is neither the result of economic, technological and social processes nor the cause of them.

The Traditional, the Modern and the Postmodern Self

Postmodernization refers to a conjunction of processes in which a series of forces from the most material to the most intellectual conjoin, inviting and demanding responses at many levels, including that of the self. We may imagine the postmodern self as the command centre of a global project, receiving and having to manage responses to a vast variety of inputs, but in the end having to take responsibility for the outcome. Sharing this problem of management may be significant others, friends, colleagues, neighbours, lifestyle or group members, but no others can relieve the self of responsibility and necessity of self-management, or enter completely into the decision-making centre. How this compares broadly to the self's position and role in the medieval and modern worlds is instructive.

In feudal societies the self was located firmly in the local and parochial structures provided by the village or town. Sources of socialization were few, predominantly the family, the estate, the village and the church, but, being all funnelled through a Catholic Christian world picture, the chances of reproduction of incongruence were small. Lacking means of communication from the outside world, as pictures, books and reading skills were rare, the production of alternative narratives of self and reality was minimal. Where such readings arose it was hard to hide and only geographic isolation or the closed communities of religious or knightly orders provided cover. Heresies were many but they orbited close to the dominant world picture of the feudal Christian order. The self was pictured as a spiritual core owned by God inhabiting a temporal body and a world inviting sin. The self's job was to manage this dilemma with the aid of prayer, the church and inherited parochial values. Above all the medieval self was other-regarding and had to keep itself pure for other reasons than selfish ones. This produced a patchwork quilt of particular social and self forms that belied all attempts at universalization and which located the self within narrow, shallow and local limits.

In the modern world, as Weber (1968) and Henry Maine (1917) tell us, the self becomes subjected to a series of forces that produces a self more universalized, rationalized and self-regarding. Modern selves are located at the centre of a more standardized and efficient regional and national set of structures provided increasingly by towns and cities. Socialization is still channelled by the family, community, class and church, but the messages are routinized and co-ordinated by the state's monopolization of tutelage. With the printing presses, both texts and pictures could be produced and reproduced for educated audiences. Improved travel took selves to sites of knowledge and knowledge to sites of selves. The production, reproduction and consumption of alternatives of self and reality multiplied, problematizing the control of knowledge for both the Catholic church and – later – the state.

The production of new and more rational narratives of self, class and reality became a necessity to provide coherence, witnessed not only in political ideologies and philosophies but also in scientific accounts of the body, mind and the commonwealth. The dominant idea of the spiritual core to the self was either forced to cohabit with materialism, as with the Cartesian systems, or to submit to it, as with Hobbes and later Marx. The modern self, then, is pictured as more materialistic, utilitarian and self-directed. Rigorous self-management is considered essential both for religious and economic reasons in Protestantism and the self-narrative is more inner-directed. But the spread of the capitalist mode of production, class-based division of labour, the civilizing processes, the Protestant work ethic, state education and welfare, and national mass forms of communication and information produced more national, universal, stratified, mass and rationalized forms of self.

The postmodern self is less securely located than its

predecessors, being located at the complex intersection of a more pluralized set of localities, a devolved set of nationalities and an all-pervasive set of international and transnational structures and sources of provision. When deemed relevant, socialization comes more pervasively from the globalized media and – increasingly – from the Internet; a socialization that escapes the nation states' capacity and will to control. As we saw in the previous chapter, the mediazation process added new areas of knowledge, which had indeterminate, plural and yet cumulative effects, not least upon the self. At the same time the connectedness of individuals and groups to the life-world of general society was loosening, if not being severed, in a process known as 'individualization' (Beck 1992; Laermans 1992: 63–72; Jagodzinski and Dobbelaere 1995: 80–81; van Deth 1995: 2).

The production, reproduction and consumption of self-narratives has blossomed in a way and to an extent that was previously unimaginable, witnessed in the thousands of items available on the shelves of every newsagent and within the covers of most of those products. Through this enlargement of sources of the self, the very possibility of mass self-production, -reproduction and -consumption is diminishing, whether at the level of class, gender, the national or the international.

The cumulative effect of these processes results in an odd historical situation where the self can gain reflexivity or awareness of itself and its sources; disembeddedness or release from some or all traditional boundaries; and a capacity and desire to make itself from the diverse and often fragmented sources and resources it has available. A self that finds itself in this position, with these experiences, resources and orientations we call *an expressive self*. Of course, not all selves in the late twentieth century can stake a claim to this position. Not all citizens in Western Europe are postmodern in our view. Many selves are still embedded in class, gender and racially dominated situations where reflexivity and the resources for self-expression are marginal or non-existent. Many other people, if not most, live in mixed positions where some of these qualities exist in some form, but not to the extent to empower or enable expressivity. We will argue, however, that more and more people in Western Europe may be characterized as expressivists, that is, as having a postmodern self.

Expressivism

By expressivism we mean the desire and capacity to actualize self-constructions or -identities. Why choose this term, what are its lineages, and what traditions, texts and movements have informed our judgement? Expressivism has the advantage to us of capturing several of the aspects of the postmodern self that we identify above. It does not capture all but enough to signal a meaning that a contemporary reader can identify. Our approach here will utilize the language game model advanced by the later Wittgenstein (1958) rather than a philological or historical model. We look in passing at the terms 'express', 'expression', 'expressionist', 'expressive' and 'expressivist'.

Several uses of the term 'express' are still current, one of the most common being a verb with reference to an emission, say of milk from a breast. In this usage it refers to putting something out as opposed to taking something in. In the terms of grammar, to express refers to the making of a statement, but more definitely the making of a clear and forceful statement. To express may here refer to a verbal, a written or a thought statement. It may also refer to a non-verbal statement in an understood sign system and vocabulary. So a footballer may express dissent at a referee's decision by a hand gesture, turning his back or looking to the heavens. A weaker and more general use of express means to speak or signal something without the notion of it being clear and forceful. However, the reference to force is carried over in the usage involving the forcing of a fluid out of or through another vessel, as when we force boiling water or steam through coffee and a coffee-making machine. Similarly, express has a use as an adverb to describe the real or metaphorical speed of something, say a train or a mail service.

Expression is most commonly used as a noun to refer to the thing expressed, namely a word, statement or signal. Originally limited to a verbal statement, it has become operable in regard to written or thought statements. Another common usage is to extend this to cover any aesthetic statement, as with a painting, sculpture, play, dance or song, which signals the meaning of their authors. This has now been extended to popular cultural statements such as dress, body art, graffiti, domestic interiors, vehicles and indeed anything that can be seen as a site for communicating the authors' feelings. Expression is also used to refer to a common or popular statement or aphorism, such as 'It never rains but it pours'. Expression, however, has a most common usage to refer to a forceful and clear statement, as is requested when an interlocutor asks you 'to express yourself more clearly'.

Expressionism is used as a noun to refer to a variety of aesthetic movements. The label is used variously and promiscuously through modern history, applied to a variety of Norwegian, Belgian, French, German, Austrian and American artists, actors and poets. Most commonly it refers to the art of Edvard Munch (1863–1944) in Norway; in France and Belgium to the Fauve group, which included Henri Matisse (1869–1954), Georges Rouault (1871–1958), Maurice Vlaminck (1876–1958), André Derain (1880–1954), Leon Spilliaert (1881–1946) and Albert Servaes (1883–1966), and which for a time embraced Pablo Picasso (1881–1973). The German movement, originally called 'Die Brücke' (The Bridge) included at various times Emil Nolde (1867–1956), Ernst Ludwig Kirchner (1880–1938), Erich Heckel (1883–1970), Karl Schmidt-Rottluf (1884–1936), Max Beckmann (1884–1950) and with political force Otto Dix (1891–1969), and the more infamous Austrians Wassily Kandinsky (1866–1944), Egon Schiele (1890–1918) and George Grosz (1893–1959). In America the final flourish was called 'abstract expressionism', its foremost representatives being Jackson Pollock (1912–56) and Clement Greenberg (1909–94), both key exponents of 'Action Painting'.

There do not seem to be any common origins in modern art except the engagement with the art of other cultures, especially the primitive imagery of Africa, and a conversation with the writings and thoughts of Friedrich Nietzsche (1844–1900). Like a family in which members may share some but not all features, with no one common feature being shared by all, expressionism is impossible to impose a single and simple definition upon. What we shall do here is to take those aspects of the various members and movements that indicate our needs and usage.

First, expressionists were generally opposed to the philosophy and practices of impressionism. Impressionism is a movement that tries to re-create reality by utilizing the minimal signs and sense data that are needed to fulfil a viewer's expectation or definition of a thing. So Pissarro or Seurat may provide only patterns of dots in colour and space to suggest a tree or river. The presumption is that the external world impresses or imposes itself upon the sensory system in a way familiar to phenomenalist philosophy. To impress is to impose upon something, to press upon it, as with a pencil mark on paper or a candidate's ability to convince an interview panel of his or her qualities. An impression is the mark or message itself. This outer-directed world of external objects impressing themselves on passive receptors is precisely what the expressionists rejected as secondary and derivative. For them art was to express, to emit, to force out of themselves into the world something that was inside themselves. Art was expression, not impression; a creation of reality from inside rather than the re-creation of reality from outside. The water-lilies series by Claude Monet may have been transitional, for at Giverny he fashioned nature and then used this artifact as the prompt to express his personal narrative of being in the world. The movement's aim was to express inner convictions with sincerity and spontaneity. But what convictions, of what reality, and how are expressions possible?

We may focus our interpretation by looking at and replying to the critique of expressionist art provided by Hal Foster (1995: 59–64). For him expressionism was a doomed movement because its key statements of belief (expressions) were untrue and collectively fallacious. The reality, the meanings they aimed to express were, first, inner and subjective, second, immediate, and, third, incapable of communication. Using an apparently Marxist frame of reference, Foster argues that inner subjective states of mind are abstractions from and created by an external and objective reality. Second, he argues that the search for the immediate, the unconditioned, the unjudged, the inner reality not corrupted by civilization is doomed to end in failure, as in the unknowable that Immanuel Kant had discovered in his epic search for the manifold of reality. Third, according to Foster, communication presumes a language or sign system shared by others. The expressionists' search, in primitive art and symbolism, in basic colour or shape, in mythical and dream-like images, for expression of their inner subjective state will either remain a failure or succumb to the language of representation involved in all art.

Expressionists were indeed preoccupied with the interior of the psyche, being explored by Freud and Nietzsche elsewhere, but they were less the idealists committing Kantian errors presented by Foster and more existential phenomenologists illustrated by Nietzsche. They appeared to express Being and not some subjective abstraction they could not name, nor the Kantian manifold. Most of the expressionists did use the term 'immediate' to try to capture the experience and the effect they were after, but this does not necessarily imply the same usage as found in Kantian metaphysics. Even if it were, by 1900 idealist philosophers had progressed beyond Kantian subjective idealism to its more objective and absolutist variants, on the one side, and to personalism, on the other, none of which suffered the problem of a purely subjective and unknowable absolute. As the major source for inspiration was Nietzsche, who was not an idealist, the immediate should be understood in a different way, as the fundamental drives for selfhood that govern human life. The feeling of Being as such was the driving force behind the remarkable series of expressions of emotions by Edvard Munch, the most famous being *The Scream*.

Finally, the expressionists' attitude to representation and language was a fundamental challenge to the prevailing artistic traditions of the West until then, but communication was not conceived by them as being without language, inexpressible and purely private. Both the movement and its members saw their engagement as public and indeed political; they sought to express and accepted that they must use a language and vocabulary. Where they differed was in the language and vocabulary in which they sought the effect; in their use of bold blocks of vivid colours and of simple but dominating shapes from circles to cubes, and in their vocabulary taken from primitive peoples they considered to be closer to nature.

Expressionism as a movement, then, was about creating – not copying or reproducing – reality, using sources of the self, communicated through a novel vocabulary using a mixture of old and new languages. It aimed to tap Being but it knew that artefact and representation were their only means to achieve its expression. Like most uses of 'express' and 'expression', they intended to make statements that were clear and forceful, as well as dramatic. Expressionists, like expressions, could communicate many things and activities, but at heart was the delving below the rational and the civilized; to break out of the bonds of the conventional, and to find and then emit and trigger the emotions, sexual passions and appetites, the desires and fears, that drive selves and humankind in their efforts to live in and to control their world.

Our use of expressivism differs from expressionism in several crucial ways. Expressionism was trying to tap some basic phenomenological features of Being believed to be shared by all human beings. Expressivism refuses to embrace this presumption of some ultimate, foundational, basal, essentialist and above all shared phenomenological reality and core to the self in the contemporary world. Selves are constructed from resources and sources that are contingent on the particular space (local/global) and time (present/future) inhabited by a particular group. Expressivism becomes understandable through what we have learned about the locality of meaning from Wittgenstein on language and from the French poststructuralists on the subject and discourse, especially Michel Foucault and Jacques Derrida (Boyne 1995). Meaning, we learn, comes from location within a particular language game and is not some essential vocabulary, and the self is constructed within discourses, some provided by others and reworked, but some being self-generated and -produced.

What expressivism shares with expressionism is deeper and wider. It shares the idea that the intention is to express what we are and want to be and not to try to copy or replicate what conventionally is and has been. Next, it aims to create a new way of being as well as a new way of looking that replaces the old and the conventional. It aims to shape the self and social reality in a fashion that is familiar and close to what you feel you are and want to be. Expressivism as a movement attracts people who are secure in their capacity to create themselves and their lifestyles from available resources and who eschew the reproduction of the existing. Like expressionism, expressivism seeks to make bold, clear and forceful statements about what its authors feel, knowing that each author may have a unique self-narrative to tell. We contend that much of postmodern art and architecture illustrates the expressivist turn as described here.

Expressivism, then, is the attitude, approach and movement of people in postmodernity who seek to pool and perm an identity for themselves and to act, behave and structure their world in order to conform to this identity. In short, it is the orientation to life of those people who like to do it for themselves, who see their lives as a voyage of discovery and a narration of self. Living within the expressivist frame is about being an impressario, for self and for others, in one's various lifestyles and occupational groupings. Such selves were discovered by Robert Bellah and his colleagues (1985) when studying new religiosity and religious pluralism in America. Expressivists were those religious people who sought and created their own forms of religion, gospel, beliefs and practices of worship. Dissatisfied with the traditional forms of worship and determined to create a form that captured their own individualized and unique sense of spirituality, they either worshipped at home or, seeking a sense of togetherness, set up their own group or cult (Jagodzinski and Dobbelaere 1995: 115, 220). We are seeking to widen this application here to include many other kinds of people and concerns than Americans and religion.

Expressivists are people who feel confident about shaping their own identity. They exhibit a high regard for their own freedom; a capacity and power to realize their projects of self-creation. These are not just individualized people left alienated or anomic, but assertive people who feel that their lives and activities can be of worth and value. Expressivists will exhibit high levels of autonomy and a capacity for self-direction, but will both welcome and be highly capable of networking and creating groups that service and realize their ambitions. Such people are at home in numerous social locations and roles, being adaptable and flexible, but they will be especially comfortable in cosmopolitan surroundings where their special skills and attributes can be fully expressed.

As should be understood from the discussion above, not everyone is as likely to become an expressivist. A high regard for one's own capacity is needed, and that regard is typical for people who feel their lives are going in the right directions, both professionally and socially. A stimulating job, with opportunities for both self-realization and self-expression, as well as supportive friends, are important components. This means that social position is an important predictor of expressivism (high position in social space), but even more important is the feeling of belonging to a group with a positive trajectory within social space. In this respect, expressivists are more likely to be common among the new middle classes than among other groupings.

Accepting and welcoming change and eschewing security, expressivists will be able to handle risk. Restlessness with the status quo we consider to be a feature of expressivists, who are always anxious to find new ways of being and living. Expressivists will be eclectic both in the sources that constitute them and in their mode of expression, mixing the traditional with the modern, the material with the spiritual, the old with the new, and the familiar with the strange, in their lifestyles and habitus. Very generally, while they will set store on the resources necessary to allow self-creation and -expression, expressivists will pay the highest regard to what Bourdieu (1984) labels cultural capital accumulation. Immediate satisfaction rather than deferred gratification is the *telos* of their lives, a job satisfaction ethic replaces the work ethic, and the boundaries of leisure, work and play are considered pervious. Hobbes would not have recognized such selves, freed of many of the insecurities he presumed, adapting to the experiences of risk and restless activity rather than seeking salvation in an ordered, secure and stable state.

Theoretical sources that have informed our account of the postmodern self and our choice of the term 'expressivism' include Charles Taylor, Anthony Giddens, William Connolly, Thomas Ziehe and Nicholas Luhmann (Gibbins and Reimer 1995: 310–312). Only Taylor uses the term, and then in two different contexts. First, he refers to the Hegelian and idealist theory of human nature in which the history of self and society is seen as the flowering and development of given impulses and potentialities. Activity is seen as the expression and realization of this potential. For us the use is related but differs. While the Hegelian conception is organic, historicist and teleological, ours is not. The sources are constructions in society, realized by emotional and intentional activity without a teleological goal or logic.

Second, Taylor argues that there are three 'sources of

the self' that have constructed modern identity: the Christian, the scientific and the romantic. Of these three, the romantic movement is tied to expressivism (Taylor 1989: 495–496). Like us, Taylor sees this sense of expressivism as prospering most in the contemporary world, but, unlike us, he sees it as a threat to human well-being due to its disembedding, individualizing and fracturing potential. The current of romantic self-expression does not fit well with community, which is Taylor's major concern, and therefore has either to subside or, better, to be tied into a communitarian project of romantic community rebuilding. Our criticism is twofold. First, the needs of any one community are not paramount and the dangers of subsuming the expressive individual in a communitarian order are great. While accepting the critique of liberalism espoused by Taylor, we are not obliged to accept the law of the excluded middle and opt for its binary communitarianism (Avineri and de-Shalit 1992; Kymlicka 1990; Mulhall and Swift 1992; Sandel 1982). We are embedded beings whose selves and identities are constructed within the groups to which we belong. However, these groups can be many and overlapping, and no one community can demand our absolute and exclusive loyalty.

Postmodern individuals learn to juggle, perm and accommodate a variety of overlapping communities and identities, some of which are traditional and many of which are artificial. Taylor is committed to the idea that only membership of an exclusive community can provide the necessary good that can generate human flourishing, whereas we argue that overlapping plural allegiances are both common and productive of psychic and social well-being. Jeffrey Weeks (1995) and Juliet Mitchell (1990), for instance, not only recognize the restructuring of the family, and see the value of new 'alternative families', but expand upon the very defects of the traditional family that are the unpleasant side of exclusive communities – patriarchy, inequality, intolerance, authoritarianism and violence. Families of choice, as they call them, which include friendship networks, neighbourhood groups and gay and lesbian couples and communes, provide networks that are often more intimate, supportive, fraternal, responsible, flexible and tolerant than their traditional alternatives. Communitarian and traditionalist attacks upon these institutions, usually built upon a myth of the family, seem attached to an agenda that seeks to limit choice, diversity and intimacy. An exclusive subscription to a Québecois nationalist and communitarian agenda may have similar defects and dangers, for its policies for Canada threaten the freedom and autonomy of other diverse communities.

Nearest to our conception but differing in crucial ways is that of Anthony Giddens in his notion of the late modern reflexive self. Theoretically grounded in the theory of structuration, it shares with us the idea of social identity as a continuous process and one in which there is no linear causal direction. In structuration theory the structures we make become the agencies for constructing the next generation of agents, so structures reproduce agents who then re-create and then reproduce structures in an endless process of modification (Giddens 1984). In the historical context of late modernity we get a process of structuration called reflexive modernization in which a number of the processes we have described above are paramount. Greater levels of knowledge flow driven by new technologies are producing a 'runaway world' in which modernity's promise of a world in control is unhinged as its very forces manufacture uncertainty, risk and disorganization. At the level of the individual this is producing selves that are disembedded from traditional structures and loyalties, dislocated from traditional locations in time and space (distanciation), but empowered to be reflexive by new knowledges and technologies (Giddens 1990; Beck et al. 1994; Heelas et al. 1995).

Giddens does not acknowledge the break with the modern self that we hypothesize. But the disembedding and reflexive processes have produced new selves at both sexual and political levels. Giddens (1992) argues that a 'transformation of intimacy' is in progress, revealing a new logic and need for intimate rather than impersonal relations between adults, both heterosexual and homosexual. Freed from the insecurity of pregnancy produced by new birth control technologies, sex becomes more about intimacy and mutual fulfilment than about the reproduction of children and society (Giddens 1991, 1992). Both gender and sexual identities become more malleable, reflexive or plastic, as individuals and groups experiment in living, and traditional sites and roles in the traditional family become disorganized (Mort 1989, 1996).

While the account of the processes of change is similar, the effects upon the self are different. For us Giddens' account is too linear and teleological; we do not see one direction of change in sexual and political identity, but a plurality of often divergent developments. Second, Giddens' view is too essentialist, as in his general subscription to the idea of a teleology of sexual emancipation – if not liberation. Emancipation and liberation are historical narratives constructed by those opposed to dominant stereotypes, but they are themselves legitimatory and regulatory discourses with problematic consequences for many. For us, sexual identities and relations are being transformed rapidly but not always in ways that can be called emancipatory.

Having now elaborated our account of the postmodernization process, the self in postmodernity, and the core concept of expressivism, we can go on to explore the implications of these for people's lifestyles, values, new politics and new social movements.

5
Lifestyle in Postmodernity

In this chapter we will deal with lifestyle choices in postmodernity. In many ways, for people living in postmodernity, the task of making decisions concerning what to do with one's life has become a more crucial part of everyday existence than it was for people living in other kinds of societies.

This has to do first of all with the fact that people now more than ever before have to take responsibility themselves for what they want to do with their lives. Traditional bonds have loosened, and it is neither necessary nor possible to automatically follow in the footsteps of one's parents. If, in traditional societies, people had few alternative life-plans to choose between, in postmodernity people have to make choices between a number of different alternatives without having the security of knowing what any of them will lead to.

Lifestyles in postmodernity are also more heterogeneous than they were in traditional societies. People today move between a number of different arenas in everyday life, and the way a person acts in one arena may have very little to do with how he or she acts in another arena.

Furthermore, lifestyle decisions to an increasing extent have become tasks that have to be carried out continuously during one's lifetime. Most people can change their lifestyles if they do not like the direction their lives are taking. It is possible to move to another place, maybe even another country; it is possible to change jobs; and it is possible to change one's leisure habits.

Being able to freely choose a lifestyle of one's liking, and being able to change that lifestyle when one tires of it, is of course an attractive notion, and for many people it is a liberating experience. However, it can also be traumatic. The security that elder generations felt has disappeared and not everyone is able to fulfil his or her dreams – partly due to the fact that not all individuals are given equal opportunities to do so.

In this chapter we will analyse the changing characteristics of lifestyle in postmodernity and we will discuss whether we are witnessing an individualization of everyday life. We will also discuss how people deal with having to take increasing responsibility for their lives.

Lifestyle: A Question of Choice

What is a lifestyle? As we define it here, a lifestyle is first of all the result of all the choices that a person makes concerning his or her life. This includes choice of work and leisure activities, but also choice of whether to live alone or not, and, if adult, whether to have children or not. Lifestyle research during the last decade has to a large extent focused upon extravagant lifestyles and on consumption; on lifestyles of people with large amounts of primarily economic but to a certain extent also cultural capital (Bocock 1992; Chaney 1996; Featherstone 1991; Shields 1992; Tomlinson 1990). This 'yuppie' focus, or, in the terminology of another discourse, this new middle-class focus, is understandable in the sense that these are lifestyles that are easy to delineate and to analyse. They also seemed to represent the era of the 1980s. However, that does not mean that other people do not have distinct lifestyles. At any given point, *everyone* has a specific, unique lifestyle, one that is similar to the lifestyle of some people, and that is quite distinct from those of others.

A lifestyle is furthermore 'visible'. A person presents himself or herself to the surrounding world through his or her lifestyle. This focus on the expressive side of lifestyle can be traced back to Veblen's *The Theory of the Leisure Class* (1899/1949). This means that the lifestyle is expressed through looks (choice of clothes and manners); but it is also expressed through actions (choice of leisure activities), objects (choice of furniture in one's home, for instance), and through the choice of friends.

Lifestyle must be distinguished from self-identity. Giddens (1991) argues that a person's self-identity takes a particular form, and that form is the person's lifestyle. This relationship should not be regarded as simple or necessary, however. Although it seems reasonable to argue that lifestyle is a material expression of self-identity, it should be noted that lifestyle has a reciprocal effect on self-identity. Pursuing a certain direction in one's life may either subtly or drastically lead to changes in one's self-identity. And people with similar self-identities may wind up with quite different lifestyles. This is due to the fact that lifestyle is about *choice* – albeit within limits. People make decisions about their lives. Not everyone has the same opportunities to choose the lifestyle of his or her dream, but then no one is totally without choices either.

People have always had lifestyles in the sense described above. Also in traditional societies, people had the opportunity to choose between alternative ways of living. However, the alternatives were for most people not that many, and they were not drastically different from each other. They did not lead to radical changes in ways of living from those of the generations preceding them either. Most people stayed put in the environment that they grew up in, and it was not unlikely for a young male to pursue the same line of work as had his father (maybe take over the family business) or for a young female to become a housewife just like her mother (maybe marrying the boy next door).

In modernity this started to change, and in post-modernity the process has accelerated. Today it is for most people highly unlikely to continue in the foot-steps of one's parents in the sense described above. First of all, many young people today do not grow up in a traditional nuclear family at all. And even if they do, it is still unlikely that they will work in the same place that any of their parents worked. That workplace may no longer exist.

Taken together, this means that people today, in the words of the German sociologist Thomas Ziehe (1986), are *culturally released*. People are set free from tradi-tional bonds and patterns of living. It is no longer possible for people to unreflexively live their lives in the way that their parents did. The decisions taken by their parents during their life course have very little relevance for the choices that they have to make.

To be culturally released is a double-edged phenom-enon. On the positive side, it means a tremendous freedom. It is not necessary to do the same kind of work that one's father or mother carried out, and it is not necessary to stay in the same place for the whole of one's life. The opportunity is given to evolve and experience things in ways unthinkable for previous generations.

But on the negative side, to be culturally released does not only mean that one gets a chance to make personal decisions. It also means that one *has* to make decisions. This is something earlier generations did not have to do (in the sense that they could continue in their parents' footsteps). And if they were to choose other alternatives, they knew much more about what the alternatives might lead to. Their lives were in many ways secure. Today that is no longer the case. People have to take responsibilities themselves, and they have to do so in a situation in which they do not know where their choices will lead them.

Furthermore, people today are more aware than ever before that there are different possible ways of living. Through travel and through the media, people know more than before about what is going on outside their immediate environment. This creates great expectations. However, not everyone is able to become what he or she wants to become, and the knowledge that there are possibilities 'out there' that one cannot reach can make the situation traumatic.

The Pluralization and Transformation of Lifestyles

The cultural release from traditional bonds discussed above concerns changes in responsibility; it concerns a change from following tradition to having to make personal choices. But there are also other lifestyle changes in postmodernity. And just as with the cultural release, these are changes that became noticeable in modernity before becoming prominent in postmodernity.

First of all, people's life-worlds have become pluralized. The concept of life-world has its origins in the sociology of knowledge tradition and it stands for the social world that each individual inhabits. Berger et al. (1974) argue that in traditional societies this world was more or less unified and integrated. Wherever an individual went, he or she was always in the same world. In modernity, and ever more so in postmodernity, this is no longer the case. The life-world has become segmented, or pluralized. Nowadays each individual has to move between a number of different arenas almost daily, both private and public ones.

Having to move between an increasing number of arenas is in itself a change from previous periods, but that is not the most important change. The drastic change is that these arenas are so different that the behaviour which is deemed valid and reasonable in one arena may not be valid at all in another arena. There is first of all the difference between how to behave in private and public arenas, but there are also distinctions within these arenas. All in all, this means that an individual's life-world today consists of a number of different 'worlds', and in these different worlds, different aspects of a person's lifestyle will come to the fore. The pluralization of the life-world thus leads to more pluralized, more heterogeneous lifestyles.

Second, we have argued that a lifestyle is the result of the choices made in everyday life. But this is always a temporary result. Individuals moving between different arenas in everyday life constantly have to make new choices. Should I change my job? Should I move? In line with making these choices, a person's lifestyle constantly changes. Sometimes the lifestyle changes subtly, sometimes drastically. The main point is that the lifestyle is never static; it is constantly transformed.

Dealing with Choice

We have argued here that people in postmodernity are forced into taking responsibility for their own lives in ways not necessary before. They have to make decisions regarding their lives in a rapidly changing environment, and they are faced with an increasing number of options, offered to them via, for example, the media and the ever-growing leisure industry. They know that they are faced with numerous choices during the course of their lifetimes. They have to face many 'fateful moments', moments that are especially crucial for the rest of their lives (Giddens 1991: 112), and they know that getting through one such moment will inevitably lead to another one later on in life. They are also aware of the fact that there are no real foundations. There are no 'right' choices to be found.

How do people deal with this? First of all, it would seem as if everyday life has become more heterogeneous. When it comes to leisure activities, there are more and more alternatives to choose between, and people combine these alternatives in different ways. There is no one fashion style that dominates. Some people live traditional lives, inside a traditional nuclear family, but an increasing number of people live in other kinds of families. In other words, in postmodernity it is possible to choose between a number of different alternatives when it comes to basically everything having to do with one's lifestyle, and people, faced with these alternatives, do choose differently.

The statement above would seem to suggest that everyday life increasingly has become a matter of personal choice. That is, it would seem as if people are able to do want they want to do, and that people can become what they want to become. It would seem as if we are witnessing a process of *individualization*, as termed by the German sociologist Ulrich Beck (1992). Traditional structuring factors such as class, gender, ethnicity and age are losing their importance, and people increasingly make individual choices, based on individual interests.

We have previously argued that people increasingly are set free in postmodernity. However, this does not necessarily mean that we are witnessing an individualization process in the sense described above. It is true that people cannot unreflexively go on with their lives in ways similar to their parents. It is necessary to take on more of a responsibility. But the question is: *how* do people do this? How do people deal with the necessity of choice?

The problem with arguing for an ongoing individualization process is that such an argument tends to forget that self-identity is socially grounded and that people in times of cultural release are also social beings. It could even be argued that it is *especially* in times of cultural release that people are social beings. As we see it, the main change in everyday life in postmodernity is not one from following tradition – reflexively or unreflexively – to finding individual solutions. It is a change from following tradition to making informed, reflexive decisions within one's social and cultural context. And when making choices, people make choices that make sense to them in their concrete social and cultural situation.

This means that the lifestyle choices people make will vary widely not primarily due to differences in personal interests, but due to different experiences related to belonging to specific, concrete social and cultural environments. People growing up in similar kinds of environments and going to similar kinds of schools tend to acquire similar outlooks on life. Given one's social and cultural background, and given one's daily environment, some acts in everyday life tend to seem natural, whereas other acts don't. If you are brought up in a home in which theatre going is a regular activity, going to the theatre as an adult will seem a natural thing to do. If you are not brought up in such a home, the probability of acquiring a taste for the theatre is much smaller. It is not impossible to acquire that taste, but it is not as likely.

Thus, people have not become 'individualized' in the too simple sense described by Beck and others. But this does not mean that things haven't changed. The situation in postmodernity *is* quite different from the situation in earlier times. People may still act as social beings, and make decisions that are similar to the ones made by other people in similar situations. But that does not make everyday life in postmodernity as stable as it was previously.

First of all, there are more alternatives to choose between than ever before. Even though people make choices that are related to their position in social space, they do have more options no matter what the position. Everyday life is more heterogeneous than before. (And that is, incidentally, one of the reasons why academics may overstate the individualization hypothesis. Since it now is possible to choose between, for instance, a larger number of sports activities than ever before, it seems as if people make more personal choices than before. But these choices may be still be primarily dependent upon class, gender and ethnicity, for example.)

Second, people move between an increasing number of different arenas regularly, and they change social and cultural contexts more often than before: people change jobs, they move to new cities, they change hobbies. In so doing, they meet different people with different experiences, and they get new outlooks on life.

Third, in a fast-moving society, with increasing contacts not only between people within one specific country but also between cultures, the bonds that structure everyday life behaviour become increasingly complex. If in traditional societies class, gender and age were primary determinants of lifestyle, in modernity, and to an even greater extent in postmodernity, other determinants also have to be taken into account, such as ethnicity and religion. Social space has become increasingly multidimensional.

Taken together, this means first of all that people in postmodernity, just like in modernity, make lifestyle choices within a structure not of their own making. And within this structure, the choices available to each individual are to a great extent dependent on that individual's position within the structure. Second, given the increasing number of visible, more or less 'attainable' options, and given the increasing pluralization of everyday life, including increasing number of contacts with different people, there is today an increasing awareness that life may look differently, and that life may be changed. People look at different options, they discuss them with friends and they reflect upon them. Every option may not be possible to attain, but that may not stop individuals from reaching after them. There is a tension inherent between what a person does, and what he or she would like to do, a tension never felt by so many people before.

How do people handle this tension? First of all, it is necessary to remember that people belong within structures, and that these structures are both enabling and constraining. They can be both enabling and constraining for the same person, obviously, but primarily structures are more enabling for some people than for others. Social space is structured in dominance, and the higher you are positioned in social space, the more power you have over your own life – the more you are enabled by the structure, generally speaking.

It is in this context that Michel de Certeau (1984) has made the highly influential distinction between strategies and tactics. People with power over their lives utilize strategies. They plan their lives according to these strategies, and they have the power to make their strategies work. They do not succeed all the time, of course, but even in the cases when they don't, they have the power to rethink and redeploy their strategy.

People with less power over their own lives cannot utilize strategies since they do not have the power to make the strategies work. Instead they have to rely on tactics. They live in a world not of their own making and they are placed in positions that they have not chosen themselves. Given these facts, they have to make the best possible of the situation. They cannot threaten the system within which they exist in a confrontational manner, in all-out war. What they *can* do is, to use a phrase of de Certeau's, to conduct 'guerrilla warfare'. This means using the consumer society, and the products of that society, in the best possible ways; in ways that may not have been the intended ones. This may mean, for instance, to use shopping malls as places to spend one's days pleasurably, without ever buying anything. It may also mean making statements with consumer products (showing opposition symbolically by disfiguring one's clothes). And it may mean getting other kinds of pleasures out of the mass media output than those intended by the creators (cf. Fiske 1989; Silverstone 1994).

It is not necessary to endorse de Certeau's views on strategies and tactics fully. His ideas of guerrilla warfare are somewhat romanticized. And it is definitely not the case that most people positioned low in social space see their everyday lives as fought out against more powerful enemies. For most people, everyday life is more mundane than that, and it is lived out in a non-confrontational way.

However, what de Certeau is correct in is arguing that people's possibilities in everyday life do vary in ways that are not random, and that the responses people can make to a great extent depend on their positions in social space. To that extent, the strategy/tactics distinction is a useful one.

The Field of Lifestyles in Postmodernity

In the preceding discussion, we frequently utilized the concept of social space, a concept heavily associated with Pierre Bourdieu. Applying his concepts in this context is, of course, not especially controversial. His work on lifestyles, primarily *Distinction* (1984), is without a doubt the most influential in the area. We will here briefly introduce his way of thinking.

According to Bourdieu, social space is built up on the basis of *capital*. The more capital you have, the higher you are positioned in social space. Social space is not one-dimensional, however. Bourdieu makes a distinction between economic and cultural capital. Economic capital is primarily, but not exclusively, material, whereas cultural capital is primarily, but not exclusively, mental. Both types of capital are important, but most people tend to acquire one of the two types.

Bourdieu argues that people positioned closely to one another in social space have many things in common, even though they may never have met. Their life experiences are similar, they have similar value systems – and they have similar lifestyles. That is, people positioned similarly in social space tend to acquire similar tastes. Bourdieu makes this explicit by arguing that it is possible to imagine a field of lifestyles that corresponds to social space. In his analyses, he shows that people with high amounts of economic capital and low amounts of cultural capital tend to have similar tastes and distastes, and thereby similar lifestyles. Their lifestyles are quite different from those of people with high amounts of cultural capital and low amounts of economic capital, and, correspondingly, from those of people with other combinations of capital.

Bourdieu's empirical analyses are primarily focused on France in modernity (in the case of *Distinction*, France of the 1960s), but, as we see it, his way of thinking is relevant also for analyses in postmodernity. First of all, the important point about Bourdieu's work is that he brings a sociological understanding of lifestyle into focus, an understanding that is just as necessary for analyses of postmodernity as for modernity (cf. Featherstone 1991). His work stands in opposition to simplified notions of increasing everyday life individualization, and he relates people's lifestyle choices to their positions in social space. He does not deny that people can move in social space, upwards or downwards (or sideways). On the contrary, social space is a dynamic space with constant movements for both individuals and whole groups of individuals. However, these movements are more or less likely depending on where you start and where you want to go. It is probable that some individuals at a given time from a particular point in social space may increase their capital drastically and move upwards, but it is highly improbable that most individuals from that point will do so.

As we see it, capital, social space and the field of lifestyles are relevant concepts in analyses of lifestyles in postmodernity also. However, what is important to emphasize is that both social space and the field of lifestyles in postmodernity, as discussed earlier, have become more complex.

In Bourdieu's conceptualization, social space in modernity is two-dimensional. It is based on economic and cultural capital, indicated primarily by occupation (he actually argues that social space is three-dimensional in the sense that time adds a third dimension, but at any given point in time, and in each concrete visualization, it is two-dimensional). It may first of all be questionable whether economic and cultural capital are the two kinds of capital that best capture the composition of social space in postmodernity, and if those two kinds suffice. What is quite clear, however, is that occupation alone is not a good indicator of capital. That was arguably not the case in modernity, and it is definitely not the case in postmodernity.

The way of defending the use of occupation as an indicator of capital is to argue that other significant factors, such as age, gender, class and education, are contained within the indicator of occupation. That is to a certain extent correct. The probability of becoming, for instance, a university professor or a psychiatrist depends largely on the above-stated factors. But that doesn't mean that their importance can be restricted to their leading to a certain occupation. It does make a difference in itself whether university professors are primarily male or female, or whether they primarily come from the working or middle class. And with the increasing movements between cultures that characterize postmodernity, factors such as ethnicity and religion problematize the composition of social space even further.

When it comes to the fields of lifestyles, in postmodernity these fields first of all have to contain many more different lifestyles than in modernity. This is the pluralization of lifestyles discussed earlier. Second, lifestyles change fast in postmodernity. Both of these factors, of course, make the fields more complex than ever before.

But another characteristic of the fields of lifestyles is that in postmodernity they tend to become more similar to each other in different countries. A field of lifestyles will obviously always have a look that is historically and culturally specific; two fields are never identical. However, in postmodernity, with increasing contacts between cultures, the same practices tend to become popular in different countries. This is related to the question of globalization and cultural imperialism taken up in Chapter 2. The practices that cross borders tend to originate in, or at least take the route via, dominating countries, primarily the United States. But it is important to remember that any imported practice will always take a culturally specific form; a form that makes sense within the culture.

Expressivist Lifestyles

A key characteristic of the field of lifestyles in post-modernity is that it contains what may be termed expressivist lifestyles, that is, lifestyles corresponding to the expressivist character of the postmodern self discussed in the previous chapter. These lifestyles are typical of people trying to create something both exciting and rewarding of their lives. The lifestyles are characterized by being highly flexible and dynamic; old distinctions – between, for instance, work and leisure, self-expression and collective work, and high culture and popular culture – break down.

In writing that self-identity corresponds to a certain lifestyle, we do not mean that there is a necessary and automatic relationship between self-identity and lifestyle. Lifestyles are always about choice. Instead, we mean that people try to express who they are or whom they want to become through the choice of lifestyle, and in that sense people with expressivist selves will most likely choose lifestyles that may be considered to be expressivist (and obviously the choice of lifestyle will then have a reciprocal effect on a person's self as well).

However, the spread of expressivist lifestyles cannot be understood solely by looking at the relationship between self and lifestyle. Just wanting an expressivist lifestyle is not enough in order to develop one. The material conditions must also be there. And those conditions are much more present in postmodern than in modern society. That is, in postmodern society, the possibilities and alternatives for developing fast-changing and flexible lifestyles are there for people who want to – and are able to – take advantage of them.

As we outlined in the previous chapter, expressivism is a movement that attracts people who are secure in themselves. But we do not mean that in a psychological or individualistic manner. In order to obtain this security, and in order for expressivism to make sense, what is needed is a belonging to a social and cultural context within which that security, and the interest in expressivism, may be developed.

Which are those contexts? Postmodern society is a society of signs and images. It is a society in which the leisure and the culture industries are booming, and it is primarily within these sectors that one may find people with expressivist lifestyles. These lifestyles are especially common among people belonging to what is alternatively named 'the new middle class', 'the new service class' or 'the new petite bourgoisie' (Bourdieu 1984; Featherstone 1991; Lash and Urry 1987), a grouping consisting of people with occupations in, for instance, the media, public relations and marketing.

The fact that expressivist lifestyles – and, indeed, 'expressive communities' (Jansson 1998) – are most common among the new middle classes is not especially surprising. Working within the media or within marketing means – hopefully – addressing factors such as reflexivity on a daily basis. And by having access to the media, and by being highly visible in public spaces, this grouping also manage to make their specific interests in the 'stylization of life' into a general agenda. The new middle classes not only profess a liking for expressivist lifestyles; they also promote such lifestyles as the most attractive and desirable ones.

We wrote earlier that expressivist lifestyles are characterized by a blurring of distinctions. First of all, there is a blurring of the distinction between leisure and work. For many people, work is something you have to do in order to survive. But within an expressivist lifestyle, work must be more than that. Both leisure and work are seen as productive and constructive parts of everyday life. Work, as well as leisure, has to be mentally and socially rewarding. This may mean obliterating the distinction between the two domains as much as possible, spending one's free time with people from work (since the interests are shared) as well as working at home (which becomes easier to do with the help of new communication technologies).

Second, an expressivist lifestyle tries to hold together an interest in self-expression with an interest in other people and in networking. This may seem a difficult thing to do, but the point is that a completely rewarding life cannot be lived by giving up the one for the other. It is necessary both to fulfil one's inner ambitions – to not give up one's personal dreams – as well as working with others in different, often rapidly changing contexts.

Third, a similar blurring concerns the relationship between high culture and popular culture. This blurring of boundaries is of course often discussed in relation to postmodernity and postmodernism. This can be seen quite clearly by looking at cultural products. High culture artists employ ideas from popular culture and vice versa, and the whole genre of info-tainment points to the blurring of fact and fiction. But the idea also extends to the people consuming the products. It is argued that in postmodernity people are no longer interested in either high culture or popular culture. In postmodernity people easily move between, and combine, these two kinds of cultures.

We think this is correct, but not in the general way it often is portrayed. In the same way as it is very difficult to blur the distinction between work and leisure unless you have a job that makes such a blurring possible, it is also difficult to move between high and popular culture unless you feel at home within both cultures. It is once again necessary to emphasize that people make choices that make sense to them in their concrete situations. The mere fact that in theory it is possible to take part in a number of different activities, and to construct a lifestyle with both high culture and popular culture elements, does not mean that most people will do so. The majority of people combining high culture and popular culture into what could be termed postmodern – or expressivist – lifestyles are those who have grown up and continued to be part of environments in which these elements seem 'natural'.

This means that people combining high and popular culture must have had access to both kinds of culture, and this obviously restricts the number of possible practitioners. High culture in modernity was generally speaking restricted to people with higher amounts of cultural capital, and popular culture was, again generally speaking, primarily consumed by people with lower amounts of cultural capital (people with higher amounts of cultural capital have traditionally shown distaste towards popular culture).

90

In postmodernity this *has* broken down, but not on all fronts. What has happened is primarily that younger well-educated people working with signs and images have started to show a taste for both high and popular culture. For these groups, a combination of popular culture and high culture seems natural; this combination has become the normal consumption pattern. For older generations with high amounts of cultural capital, and for younger generations without that capital, this is not the case. As of now, cultural capital is highly related to high culture. In the future, a knowledge of popular culture may also be needed (cf. Boëthius 1995).

The Role of Lifestyle in Postmodernity

Ever since Veblen's *The Theory of the Leisure Class* (1899/1949), the idea has been extant in academia that having a particular lifestyle may mean more than just having some particular everyday leisure interests. Having a particular lifestyle, and showing it off to other people, is a way of showing a belonging to a particular group in society, and of marking distances from other groups. And this way of marking distances, showing distinctions between groups of people, may in itself lead to the *upholding* of these distinctions. In recent writings, this argument is, of course, most forcefully put forward by Bourdieu (1984).

What happens to this crucial role of lifestyles in postmodernity? As argued above, the field of lifestyles has not turned into an 'anything goes' field where anyone chooses any kind of lifestyle. The field contains a greater number of different lifestyles but it is still structured, even though its pluralization in itself makes the

structure less visible (and leads to the debatable con-
clusions of increasing individualization).

However, the pluralization of the field has had consequences. It may not be the case that anyone can do
anything, but with such a pluralization, the hierarchy
of the field is questioned. That is, people with lower
levels of capital choose other lifestyles than people with
higher levels of capital. But if in traditional societies
and in modernity everyone within the field acknowledged that some lifestyles were superior to others
('those things are not for the likes of us'), in postmodernity that may not be the case. People with
different levels of capital have different lifestyles. But so
what? Who cares? With increasing knowledge, primarily through the media, of what other people are doing,
the aura surrounding other people's lifestyles has disappeared. The symbolic value of having one lifestyle
rather than another seems to have disappeared.

This does not mean that the role of lifestyle has
become less important in postmodernity, however. We
are arguing that the relative value of having one
lifestyle rather than another has declined in importance. And a good thing that is too. But the field is still
structured. Some groups of people have more power in
social space than do other groups of people, and the
choice of lifestyle may both increase and decrease one's
power. People positioned high in social space have the
possibility of choosing lifestyles that give them contacts with other people positioned similarly in social
space. They acquire first-hand important information
in all kinds of matters. They can choose to let their
voices be heard in debates in the public sphere. People
positioned lower down in social space have to rely on
tactics as opposed to the strategies of the powerful. This

means making the best possible of the situation, but it is not an ideal situation, and strategies that seem right and necessary at certain times may not be functional in the long run. We will return in subsequent chapters to the question of how people positioned differently in social space to different extents, and in different ways, make politics parts of their everyday lives.

6

Values, New Politics and New Social Movements

Having elaborated the new self and the new logic of cultural and lifestyle expression and accumulation, we can now move on to explore the implications of this for values and politics. The original argument for a connection between postmodernism and new politics was hypothesized by us in 1989 (Gibbins 1989a: 23–24). We argued that those citizens most in tune with postmodern culture would be those who were most likely to be involved in new political activities such as direct action and belonging to new social movements, and less likely to be involved in old political activities such as party and pressure group affiliation. In 1995 we developed the argument by looking at the creation of new selves, the multifarious value patterns they produce and their new political behaviours, and we provided some empirical evidence in support (Gibbins and Reimer 1995). Here we wish to revisit this last argument with the intention of improving the analysis, providing more illustrations and exploring deeper the implications.

Values

Values are the beliefs we have about what is good and bad. Good and bad, and the other moral binary terms in our vocabulary, such as right and wrong, just and unjust, courageous and cowardly, set the map for our moral behaviour at the individual and the group level. They also set the moral map for, and give direction to, our behaviour. This is true of moral terms in a way that is not true of non-moral terms. The major reason for this is not in their supposed ontological or metaphysical superiority, but in the use of the terms and phrases. Moral terms are primarily prescriptive whereas non-moral terms are primarily descriptive. When we use the terms 'good', 'right', 'just' or 'courageous', we indicate not only our approval but our approval that this act or class of acts should be done or resisted. When we use a descriptive term such as 'red', 'efficient', 'profitable' or 'dangerous', we do not imply that the thing, act or class of acts is something we both approve of and prescribe. In short, the defining characteristic of values is that they indicate or prescribe what we ought or ought not to do as against what is or is not the case.

Moral terms differ from others in certain crucial ways. Whereas we may give examples of the correct application of a moral term, we cannot point to an empirical or observable object, thing or behaviour. In short, moral values are unobservable (van Deth 1995: 25). Many efforts have been made to reduce or to legitimate moral claims by reference to observable and empirical objects, as when John Stuart Mill tried to establish that desirable was that which most people actually desired, but it is generally felt that such moves are fallacious (Moore 1903: 38–41, 64–70). Next, moral terms do claim some metaphysical and ontological superiority whether this can be proved or not. Hence moral terms are used in discussions rather as trump cards are used in card games; they are held to overpower or have some special and superior status over other sorts of claims, as for instance those about efficient outcomes. Because of this quality, and its power to overcome utilitarian or instrumental considerations, philosophers have often described moral values as a priori as against a posteriori, true without reference to experience as against depending for their effectiveness on experience. Whether this claim or belief can be upheld is less important here than that it is generally believed to be the case. Values therefore have a special status as action-ordering principles in political life and are therefore significant as an object for study.

Values do not exist in isolation from other sorts of preferences which may themselves influence activity. A preference for football over tennis may affect television behaviour as well as the choice of leisure sports activities. But we must be careful to separate value and non-value preferences. A value preference is one that makes an action categorical, imperative or binding, whereas an ordinary preference only makes it advisable. So the moral value preference to avoid eating animal flesh makes the practice not only objectionable but impermissible, whereas the non-moral preference for eating lamb rather than chicken does not have the effect of making lamb eating imperative nor chicken eating impermissible. Preferences express a gradation only on a scale of desire and not on the scale of the desirable, understood as something worthy of being desired. Values, on the other hand, are conceptions of the desirable defined in this way. Values are, however, often mixed with preferences, and this makes analyses more imprecise.

Many studies of public opinions around politics have been about preferences which are revealing in terms of a shift to postmodernism, but those are not the centre of this study, which concentrates instead upon value preferences. Similarly, 'attitude' is a general term referring to a whole array of desires, fears, inclinations and preferences. Amongst or in our attitudes are many non-moral and non-value preferences and inclinations, for example an inclination to prefer a present to a less secure future satisfaction. Moral attitudes differ in being those that have imperative, categorical and prescriptive elements. Most general attitude systems are driven by value preferences (Klages and Herbert 1983; van Deth 1995: 32–33).

Values are rarely held in isolation by a person; it would be rare to find someone with just one or a random set of values. Instead values are usually mixed and permed together in what political scientists call value orientations, or what philosophers may call value or ethical systems, patterns of belief, or moral theories. We are less concerned with these systematically related theories and especially not second-order reflections on them, namely ethical systems or moral philosophies. We are concerned with first-order value preferences and value orientations, the latter being defined as more or less regular patterns of value preferences over time. As with many other things, when a collection is brought together and ordered it has greater weight and effect than when separate elements are considered either alone or in aggregate. Hence value orientations are considered to have greater potential for political effect than any one value or aggregate of values.

Postmodern Value Orientations

Postmodern value orientations are very different from all other value orientations considered by political scientists and theories. They differ in levels of generality/

specificity, in ordering principle and in stability, over both time and space. Feminism, environmentalism, libertarianism, materialism and postmaterialism can all be contrasted with postmodernism on these criteria. First, all of the above refer to specific value patterns; hence feminist values include a preference that women ought not to be subordinated, treated as unequal and that they ought to be treated as independent and be encouraged to participate in politics (Lundmark 1995). In contrast, postmodern value orientations have no specific value preferences except at the most general level, that is, a general belief that every person ought to able to be what they want to be. In this sense postmodernism is less an orientation and more of a loose-knit ordering or patterning system whose only major and essential rules are that everybody should order their values, value preferences and attitudes for themselves. Whereas environmentalism demands subscription to a core set of values ordered around some ground norms such as 'We ought to save the earth', postmodernism refers to no core values – no ground norms – and sets autonomy or self-authorship as its only main principle.

Left materialists are expected to hold core values together and not easily let essential socialist principles such as public ownership lapse. Postmodernists, on the other hand, are happy and indeed keen that individuals and groups will continue to explore and restructure their value patterns, allowing great variety, eclecticism and personal patterning with little fear of abandoning traditional principles (bricolage, à la carte values). The same is true for value patterns over time. While postmaterialism requires that a generation socialized into a particular set of values keep these for life, be it self-realization, greenness or feminism (Scarbrough 1995:

124–128), postmodernism instead hypothesizes that socialization is a continuous process and that post-modernists will regularly restructure their values. Finally, other value dimensions are considered to be of universalistic application to other parts of the world (Inglehart and Abramson 1994: 347). Postmoderniza-tion is considered to be of universal application as a process but it is considered that *de facto* each society, group and individual will construct its/his or her own and ever-changing value orientation.

Our hypothesis and theory of value change, then, is unique not only in content but also in form. We not only construct a new value dimension, hypothesizing a major shift from modern to postmodern value orienta-tions, but we consider this to mean a movement from value orientations that are specific, unified and stable in order over time and space, to a new value orientation where none of these apply. By a postmodern value ori-entation we mean a system that is only barely patterned. It is a general ordering principle that allows any number of specific values, in any range or permu-tation, for a variety of groups to order and disorder, keep or change, spread or keep parochial as they wish. By using the metaphor of the Internet or the World Wide Web we may say that postmodernism requires only that users conform to a minimal set of operating instructions or Netiquette, and that what they do with the Net, how it is used, operated and extended to the outside world, is a matter for the users and not the Net providers. Postmodern value orientations are held together with an ordering system more like a web than a building or body.

Postmodern selves will pool values as they pool everything else in their lives on the operating principle of expressive cultural accumulation. Adopt, pool and apply the values that best express what you feel best suits your understanding of yourself and your group. A postmodern value orientation, then, is rather like a postmodern habitus, carefully and purposively created to reflect the notion of self invoked. These values will be blended together with other preferences and attitudes to create a lifestyle.

What general features will postmodern value orientations exhibit? They will be self-fashioned, pooled and permed from a variety of sources. They will be highly differentiated in design, mixing old and new in eclectic forms, and they will be individualized or personalized even when the value orientation is shared by a group.

Pooling and perming means selecting your own version from a list of available sources, as in score draws in football pools or lottery numbers. A postmodernist self may select a collection of values that would be considered anarchic or perverse by modernists. Hence a feminist may mix her value of female self-determination with a lesbian value to only have sex with other women, with a value that monogamy is the antithesis of desired freedom and that she would not date anyone who eats meat. No conventional moral belief system could begin to understand, let alone know how to evaluate, such an orientation.

Differentiation in design means that each self or group will seek to set its values in distinction to those of others. This was the finding of William Connolly in his study *Identity/Difference: Democratic Negotiations of Political Paradox* (1991). Whereas in conventional modern belief systems identity was fashioned by membership of large collectivities that differentiated themselves from other large collectivities, the logic of postmodern affiliation is to fashion one's own identity as a response to other individuals and groups to which you have relative proximity (Gundelach 1992: 317–318). Hence in postmodernity you are more likely to feel a sense of injustice through what Runciman (1972) calls relative deprivation, not doing so well as a colleague, rather than absolute or universal deprivation of not doing so well as others in an occupational hierarchy.

Individualizing and personalizing refer to the processes in which postmodern selves adopt and adapt values to fit their particular subjective needs. Here a good example is the case of Catholics who, while still subscribing to the formal values of the Ten Commandments and the values decreed by the Pope, feel able to abridge, modify and amend these to allow for such sexual options as birth control, adultery and divorce, and such non-sexual options as non-atten-dance at church and confession and belonging to a communist organization for liberation in Latin America. Personalizing is taken from the popular cul-tural phenomenon of adapting a mass-produced icon into something recognizable as your own. So a cult car such as a Volkswagen Beetle can have any number of modifications to colour, wheels and sound system to express the owner's personality, and the value system of a postmodern feminist can be tweaked by cross-dressing or adopting the hairstyle of Marilyn Monroe. A personalized value system is one in which your ver-sion of feminist Buddhism is modified by a value preference for non-penetrative tantric sex in a public rather than private space.

One of the most profound differences between post-modern and other value orientations is their inclusivity. Whereas most value systems are exclusive and demand adherence to most values by its members, adherents to a postmodern value orientation can mix and match their values in a more or less never-ending set of possible permutations. Not only this, but they can mix and match old and new values, as when an expressive search for vegetarian food options becomes mixed with a modern acquisitive materialist instrumental imperative to own the recipe books of famous vegetarians from history. Not only can modern values be mixed with the postmodern, but a postmodernist orientation can envelop particular industrial and green, male and feminist, materialist and postmaterialist, and authoritarian and libertarian values.

All of these compositional qualities can be considered to be defects by adherents of modernist and other value orientations, because they encourage and create divisions, difference, instability, confusion, possible dissonance and incommensurability, both in the selves and groups and in the value patterns themselves. An alternative is to see these very qualities as strengths which allow for widespread and deep feelings of congruence and attachment. Postmodernists want to feel at home and at ease with their values and lifestyle, wanting now the sort of synthesis of self and other, subjective and objective, morality and freedom that Hegel believed was only possible in the future absolute.

Within a value orientation are several components, including first-order values, or direct imperatives such as moral rules like the Ten Commandments; some value preferences, such as the general value that we ought to encourage freedom or rights; and some second-order rules and principles. A second-order value means a background managing or organizing principle that governs first-order rules and preferences, such as the principles of toleration and freedom of expression. A postmodern value orientation differs from modern and traditional orientations by the balance and relationship between these components. Postmodernists have the fewest first-order categorical imperatives or rules possible, so maximizing the arena for freedom of choice of other values and the rights and potential for their expression. They will try to limit even value preferences to a minimum for the same reasons, while accepting that some of these will be necessary if one's actions are to have a moral normative structure. This balance leads to actual or potential instability in a postmodern value orientation, as if we had a highway code organized mainly on advice about good driving habits rather than specific advice upon rules of the road. We recognize the need therefore for postmodernist ethics to have some few but basic second-order value principles or *principles of a postmodern political ethics*. These will be elaborated in Chapter 8.

Who amongst contemporary populations in Europe shares the postmodern value orientation? Our empirical research confirmed our hypothesis that we would find a small but significant and growing percentage of citizens with this orientation (Gibbins and Reimer 1995: 317–320). While evident in all countries, the growth was most pronounced in northern Europe, especially Holland and Sweden. The young and highly educated were the most postmodernist, with the proportion rising the further citizens ascended into the education systems. Access to additional forms of communication systems correlated with postmodernism, it being most pronounced with those who had access to television sets, videos and computers. Those who had travelled abroad were also more inclined towards postmodernism.

All in all, the results suggest that postmodern value orientations *are* on the rise in Western Europe. And the results also show how dependent they are on structural factors. The value orientations are most common in the most (post)modernized countries, and within each country, the value orientations are most common among people with high amounts of cultural or economic capital.

Postmodern Values and Political Behaviour

How do postmodern values relate to political behaviour in Western Europe? Postmodernists, we asserted, are those who seek both to express their own pool of values and preferences, and to do so in their own ways. We found that postmodernists participate in some ways that are different to modernists, especially in favouring more expressive direct action and grass-roots activities, routed if at all via new social movements rather than via conventional political parties and interest groups. While still participating in conventional politics, postmodernists understand this in a more detached and sceptical way than modernists and combine and reinforce this with a range of alternative activities.

In modernity political behaviour was routinized into a series of mass participatory and elite management processes, generally called conventional political activity and government. Participation in conventional politics took several forms which could be presented in a participation scale: moving from the most to least common was taking an interest in politics, voting for a political party, belonging to a pressure or interest group, belonging to a party, direct action, standing for election in a political body, holding office in a political body, and being a member of Parliament (Milbrath 1965). Political protest via direct action was a rare and widely discouraged form of participation.

Modernization was already beginning to disrupt old values as well as allegiances to, and trust in, political bodies. Postmodernization has continued the process to a point where we can speak of the dealignment of voters and parties, decrease in depth of allegiance or salience, dissonance in regard to ideology, volatility in allegiance and participation, incivism and growth of distrust, declining attachment to and felt legitimacy of the state, and increasing cynicism and political alienation. We can also witness a redirection of political effort and a general realignment in politics from 'old' to 'new politics'. By this we mean a gradual process of societal redirection towards a range of new interests, attachments, alignments, memberships, participations and behaviours (Barnes and Kaase 1979; Bell 1973; Dalton 1988; Jennings and van Deth et al. 1989; Offe 1985; Touraine 1974). New political activities are not only more unconventional, involving protest activities. They are less structured, allowing more direct involvement to participants. They are less stable in membership and agendas over time. They are less related to economic and social stratification. And they are less about ideology, interest and power. New social movements, such as the peace, feminist and environmentalist movements, are seen as ideal type exemplars of this shift to new politics (Melucci 1980, 1988, 1989).

It is important to note the crucial role played by the

mass media in relation to political behaviour. Today it is primarily through the media that people are able to make sense of politics. There are disturbing elements to this. First, as noted in Chapter 3, the media system is becoming increasingly commercial. It is important to reach the biggest audience possible, and to do it fast. Thus, the portrayals the media give of political events are often superficial. But, second, the media increasingly also shape political processes. Election campaigns are obvious examples, but also on other occasions, the role of the media is increasing, leading to doubts about the workings of democracy in contemporary Western societies (Blumler and Gurevitch 1995). However, the media are also able to focus upon political events, making them visible for larger audiences. The events at Tiananmen Square and around the Berlin Wall are two such examples, the beating of Rodney King a third. In these and other cases, the media made a significant – and valuable – contribution (Fiske 1996; Lull 1995; cf. Dayan and Katz 1992).

In relation to new social movements, it is quite clear that these in many ways are media phenomena in the sense that the movements are able to handle the media much better than are traditional political parties. By being visible, they are able to attract new members. And by promoting a different style, they also function as lifestyle markers in ways unimaginable for the traditional parties. Thus, with the help of the media, in an interesting interaction between people and the workings of the new social movements, political practices increasingly become intertwined with other lifestyle practices, blurring the distinction between politics and lifestyle.

While several social scientists have argued for this

shift from old to new models of politics, our contribution to the debate is to identify this shift as a feature of and contribution to the postmodernization of society (Gibbins 1989a; Gibbins and Reimer 1995). Our argument in this chapter is that new postmodern selves with postmodern value orientations are most likely to be attracted to new political activities. Modernists may also do so as adjuncts to old political activities, but postmodernists will do so more naturally – as the most appropriate way to express themselves.

Our major competitor in this field is Ronald Inglehart, for whom the emergence of new politics is a feature of the materialism to postmaterialism cultural shift (Inglehart 1977, 1990; Scarbrough 1995). Support for this hypothesis comes from Anthony Giddens in a recent summary (Giddens 1998, 19–21). We will distinguish our views from Inglehart by comparing them on four different levels associated with the change from old to new politics: the levels of actors, values, issues and behaviours. The changes have been interpreted by others as reflecting alterations to the economy, and to the development of disorganized capitalism and its attendant societal class cleavages (Offe 1985, 1995), but Inglehart attributes them primarily to value changes. Inglehart's hypothesis has been tested in several studies, and it has been found, for instance, that postmaterialists are more likely to engage in grassroots, protest and direct action practices. Our own study found similar connections between postmodernists and a variety of direct action behaviours (Gibbins and Reimer 1995: 322–326; cf. Jahn 1989; Schmitt 1989). Postmodernists scored equally with modernists on participation in conventional behaviours such as voting for a party, but scored higher in regard to unconventional activities such as signing a petition or attending a demonstration.

Our model and arguments can be shown to differ at the four levels identified above, and while we now find Inglehart arguing for a synthesis of the two accounts, we still feel that at the heuristic level our model has advantages.

At the level of agency or self, the postmaterialist argument judges selves to be future-driven by the goal of self-realization, while the postmodern claim is that agents are becoming more present-oriented and driven by the goal of self-expression. An animal rights protester, we argue, is driven more by the need to stop immediate suffering to animals than by the long-term goal of saving or promoting the well-being of the animal species, and does so more to express his or her disgust than to realize some permanent feature of character or personality. There is no fixed self with core values, as postmaterialists assert, but an ever-changing self with values being repositioned and amended regularly. Hence, while Giddens can envisage a 'Third Way' we hypothesize the emergence of many more distinctive ways in politics (Giddens 1998).

Postmaterialists would ascribe to a homogeneous set of values while postmodernists would ascribe to a heterogeneous set. In other words, postmaterialists would expect an animal rights protester to share in a fairly complete set of environmentalist values, whereas we would not only doubt this but would expect many of those attending a demonstration about, say, the export of live animals from Britain for battery farming production to be protesting for the first time on this issue and to not embrace a wider package of green and vegetarian values and preferences. Again we would not expect the participants in this demonstration necessarily to be the more highly educated and attuned to the cause by long-term socialization. We rather expect them to be culturally attuned and primed for action by media coverage of the event. In fact, the demonstrators at Winchelsea in southern England surprised observers with their wide range of class, occupational, gender and ethnic backgrounds. At the port of Winchelsea in 1997, demonstrators manned a permanent picket to stop the export of young veal calves to the Netherlands for fattening and slaughter. In the struggle with the police trying to assist the passage of the animals, one young woman died under the wheels of a transport lorry and numerous others were manhandled, arrested and detained. For many this was the first and perhaps only cause that could trigger such a radical political response.

On the issues agenda the repertoire is largely shared by postmaterialists and postmodernists for the 1970s and 1980s, focusing primarily on feminist, peace, environmentalist, green, animal rights and anti-racist issues. The difference is that in the postmaterialist frame the agenda is fixed for this generationalist frame but for postmodernists it is undergoing reordering and reprioritization. We consider peace movement activities to be in decline but nationalist and anti-nazi movements to be in ascendance. In the nineties a new ('third wave') feminist agenda of issues will replace the issue agendas of the seventies, and new issue areas, such as the value agenda of sexual minorities, that is, lesbian mothers and female fetishists, will be added (Flax 1987, 1993; Gamman and Makinen 1994; Gibson and Gibson 1993; Grosz and Probyn 1995; Segal 1997; Squires 1993). The rainbow alliances considered to be a feature of postmaterialist new politics we see as being replaced by paintbox alliances.

On behaviours we expect an unstable and ever-changing, often volatile, agenda. Postmodernists are excellent at adapting to situations, especially when authorities close off avenues of protest. Paul Heelas (1996) has shown how 'new agers' have responded to public order legislation aimed at restricting opportunities to meet by clogging motorways with slow-moving convoys and then forging unlikely alliances with local farmers who share their agendas and are willing to negotiate festival site usage. Gay and lesbian activists have cut down oppositional protests and boycotts in favour of more affirmative Gay Pride Festivals and the promotion of gay and lesbian banks, hotels, holidays and other dedicated homosexual services, and may organize homosexual theatrical productions for Christians in church sites. Transsexuals and transvestites may not only enter as new agents in the political agenda, with new values and a new set of issues, but they may situate their unconventional activities in public sites previously considered out of bounds, as did sadomasochists in London, who recently organized a full-day festival of promotional activities, including 'dog obedience' competitions, at a central university site. In short, the agents, values, issues and range of activities we are witnessing in new politics today break the rather fixed bounds set by postmaterialists.

Postmodernists turn out to be activists and participants, supporters of democracy with high levels of subjective confidence in being effective in politics. While distrusting conventional behaviours, they will use and operate within parties, parliaments and bureaucracies, but they are more inclined towards unconventional activities. For instance, postmodern feminists may be found in parties but are more likely to seek effective expressions by activities in women's friendship networks and in local support groups, to be vigilant activists at work, and to see politics as appropriate also in the home and in the bedroom.

At the organizational and structural levels, analysts of new politics and of postmaterialists in particular identify the new sites for activity in new social movements. Our argument differs both in that we ascribe the rise of new social movements to postmodernism and in that we see them as only one rather limited site, others being the myriad of lifestyles being created as well as the imbrication of political expression more widely into everyday life.

We have looked at four particular lifestyles across Europe to see how values mediated via lifestyle impact upon political behaviour and attitudes to government (Gibbins and Reimer 1998). Using Eurobarometer 28 conducted in 1987, we were able to identify eleven interests that citizens could combine into different lifestyles: interests in science, the arts, national politics, sports, solving social problems, foreign cultures, languages, the environment, third world politics, international politics and world peace. We looked first at the structure of lifestyles to see how pluralized they were becoming. We hypothesized that in a modern society there would be a small number of mass lifestyles, whereas in a postmodern society there would be a larger number of diverse lifestyles.

We found wide diversity in pluralized lifestyles in Europe, with Denmark, Netherlands, Germany, Italy and Greece having the most pluralized lifestyles.

Generally, the wealthier the country the more pluralized the lifestyles. Amongst individuals the higher educated had more pluralized lifestyles than the less educated, younger people more pluralized lifestyles than the older and women more pluralized lifestyles than men. It would seem that in all countries, cultural capital as indicated by level of education was the main indicator of a postmodern pluralized lifestyle.

Next we looked at how politics interact with other interests within different lifestyles. We focused upon lifestyles combining politics with sports or the arts or both (using sports as an indicator of low levels of cultural capital and the arts as an indicator of high levels of cultural capital). On the whole, we found that people with the most pluralized lifestyles – people combining politics with both sports and the arts – used the widest range of political practices. The distinction between a politics/sports and a politics/arts lifestyle mattered for one's choice of political activities. An interest in the arts is a more elite concern and it attracts activities directed to the government directly, whereas the more mass popularity of sports attracts a broader and more diverse range of activities. Arts groups tend to lobby government both direct and via the media, whereas sports groups use a wider range of lobbying measures, including pitch demonstrations. We found that those with a politics/arts lifestyle were more inclined to position themselves on the left and those with a politics/sports lifestyle to position themselves more on the right.

The form and content of lifestyles as discussed here had little impact upon trust in government and democracy. This was not a surprise as all lifestyles require the public goods that a stable and effective government provides. With the growing pluralization and diversification of lifestyles, especially alternative variants, governments are finding it easier to hold the ring between competitors, rather than trying to impose a single dominant form of life. A postmodern tolerance and even celebration of diversity along with a positive policy of enablement is indeed the only sensible strategy for the government of a society that embodies a plurality of often incommensurable lifestyles, and which wishes to engender widespread support and legitimacy.

New social movements were a phenomenon of the period from the 1960s to the present in the West. They offered a more flexible, user-friendly, mass form of democratic political body than did traditional parties and pressure groups. However, as Yeatman (1994: 113–117) argues, their real significance did not lie in what they accomplished, or in their widening of access to democratic politics to new individuals and groups, but in their *style* of politics; a style that embraces performativity and politicization. By performativity is meant a set of rhetorical practices that encourage open dialogue, discussion, dissension and the sharing of information. By politicization is meant the process by which voices may bring previously excluded issues into politics. Both reflect the key observations that as the nature, operation and agenda of politics are constituted in discourse, so the key method of political activity is voicing one's view and getting it heard. Politics in postmodernity is recognized to be constructed in language; politics *is* language.

In postmodern societies one additional feature of politics is its transnational and international dimension. In Western Europe both old and new politics are now organized transnationally at the levels of agency, values, interests and behaviour, often using information technologies as linkages. But the Internet, especially, allows for the more pluralized and differentiated lifestyle groups to compensate for the near monopoly of radio and television given to the older groups such as parties and interest groups. While transnational organizations were originally developed by such interests as drugs companies, banks and parties, with postmodernization we can find this extending to disability groups, sexual minorities and to minority sports supporters. We will develop the arguments above in Chapter 8.

7

The New State, Transnationalism and the International Order

Postmodernization and globalization processes are changing the nature of the territorial nation state as well as changing values and political institutions. In this chapter we will examine these processes and their implications for the state and its sub-system, the welfare state. We argue that the old political order around the state is melting and that the restructuring process produces a variety of interlinking and overlapping political authorities. We especially analyse the emergence of the non-territorial transnational political authority and the territorial 'new state' (cf. Gibbins 1990).

The new state is both a response to postmodern societal changes and a reaction to the external processes of globalization. Restructuring builds upon Giddens' (1984) notion of structuration. Actions, discourses and practices solidify over time into structures. However, it would be a reification to treat these as fixed. Rather, they alter or restructure as agents, and interact with the institutions through time. Structures that do not accommodate themselves to pressures may go out of existence, whereas those that do alter their shape, structure, logic and legitimacy. The nation state is the case of a central modern structure undergoing radical internal and external pressures which are forcing a variety of restructurings in response. Post-industrial theory accounts for this in terms of new technologies causing the pressure and the new technocratic state being the response (Bell 1973). Post-Fordist theory sees the new drive for profitability in a global economy as the cause (Burrows and Loader 1994). We share several notions on restructuring with Philip Cerny, in his imaginatively entitled book *The Changing Architecture of Politics: Structure, Agency and the Future of the State* (1990: 112). We diverge from his diagnosis and views in most details but we have found the theoretical paradigm and its ramifications a source of stimulation.

International and Transnational Politics

One of the most profound aspects of postmodern politics, we argued in Chapter 2, is the interconnectedness of international, national and sub-national politics, economics and culture. Not only are actors, events, structures and forces more interconnected, but there is an interpenetration at all levels from one sector to the other. We shall distinguish between international and transnational activities and processes. The international is where nation states interact. Interconnectedness occurs in a multitude of ways, and external actions have ramifications inside the state whether the state plans and agrees to this or not. The transnational is where other groups interact – whether states like it or not. The transnational is where problems and issues are shared by groups within different states, and where the processes or structures cut horizontally through the states.

With the growing reality of a shrinking world and shrinking resources, of the growing complexity of problems and the costs of their solutions, internationalism has grown in significance. States have grown to meet these challenges in a variety of ways, but few have proved to be of lasting significance. Faced with major problems on a world scale – world energy shortages, global warming and AIDS – international co-operation through such organizations as the United Nations and the International Court of Justice have been much vaunted but handicapped by the very logic and operation of the traditional nation state. Internationalism is still a relevant and justifiable ideal and process, but by itself it does not meet the needs of postmodern society and politics due to the complexities of interconnectedness, interpenetration and transnationalism.

Internationalism or intertwining arises from the need for states to co-operate in a variety of areas where complexity and cost require this, as in the need to establish a defence or trading bloc or a satellite launching system. Generally those structures which were set up to facilitate such ventures (NATO and the European Community) have proved effective and fared well with publics in Europe, but the view that their success would undermine and challenge the legitimacy and sovereignty of the state has not been proven (Kaase and Newton 1995: 102–125). It seems that whatever governments and parties say and do, citizens in Europe trust each other to the point of co-operation at numerous sub-state levels. Modernism would hypothesize the global movement to federal and international governments, but postmodernists hypothesize that practical interconnectedness and intertwining will operate without the need for such universalistic and unilinear assumptions.

Multinational corporations are the ultimate example

of transnational penetration into states forcing inter-connectedness, though other examples may prove to be of longer term significance for the state. Such examples are the growth of transnational communications and media systems, especially the Internet; world finance and banking systems; interest transnationalism evidenced in the environmental and feminist movements; transnational terrorism; and the growing significance of transnational cultures from youth, gay and feminist cultures to such pan-nationalisms and pan-religions as the Black, Arab, Islamic, Jewish and Chinese transnationalisms. Almost unnoticed, these pan-national cultures have come to have a major destabilizing impact upon many states, as evidenced in French Canada and in the case of Catholicism in Poland.

Sub-nationalism is also an observable phenomenon again after years when social scientists were fond of such phrases as the 'convergence thesis' and the 'end of ideology' (Bell 1960). While most obviously blossoming in Eastern Europe today, these sub-nationalisms have also had a major impact upon national and international politics in postwar Europe, and especially so in Spain, Britain, Belgium and France. Sub-national groups often establish transnational and even international links with other groups, avoiding intermediation by the state.

The emergence of the new world order implies the restructuring of the state and the international order – especially state diplomatic activity – in reaching solutions to interest conflicts (Giddens 1998, 144–147). Most bodies now feel they act for themselves in other countries without the need for direct national diplomatic intervention. We are witnessing the rise of intra-state

and transnational structures and solutions. The precip-
itating factors are several, including the recognition of
nation state overload and impotence in many areas,
and increasing cost of research and development of
solutions, but the major factors are the growth of international capitalism (non-pejorative), the growth of new
technologies, the realization that many problems can
only be tackled globally, the growth of global communication and culture, and the slackening of national,
imperial and even local cultures and ideological attachments (US hegemony).

Today it is almost a commonplace to speak of economic, political and cultural interdependence.
Interdependence is also accompanied by a new openness of structures to the external world. But
interdependence, globalization and the world system
are also accompanied by the weakening of nation
states and the old power-broking systems of diplo-
macy, by a recognized and declining ability of states to
solve problems by war, and the loss of superpower
hegemony, both real and cultural, all of which cause
international instability. The effects of cross-cutting
transnational factors have also eroded the unity of
states and their ability to solve interest intermediation
problems at the levels of production, social investment
and consumption, causing instability. Into the equation have come new and often less predictable actors
and structures which destabilize matters further. Once
a lone voice, Hedley Bull is now at the centre of those
who consider the world order to be in crisis or in such
rapid change that the old order is in decline and no
new order other than anarchy or polyarchy seems
credible (Brown 1988; Bull 1977; Bull and Watson 1984;
Rengger 1989).

The Modern Nation State and Sovereignty

While eschewing some of the benefits of essentialism in favour of a non-essentialist analysis of the state, we may take Weber's definition and characterization as our starting point. Our aim is to show why and how the nation state as it has been is now undergoing such a change that its identity may not allow recognition in several decades' time. An adaptation of David Held's reasoning is the easiest way to make the points. Held concludes that multinationalization of previously domestic activities, allied to globalization and inter-meshing of decision making, has 'eroded the powers of the modern nation state' (1989: 237). The effects are not uniform across existing nation states, however. States still retain enormous power, and are not all ready to submit decision making to other superior powers. In short, *de jure* claims to sovereignty are still claimed and existent alongside a gradual erosion of *de facto* power.

Sovereignty involves the possession of absolute power and authority within a given territory. The specific territory that came to locate sovereignty in the modern world was the state. For postmodernists the state is a historical construct, a historical house constructed in part from the remnants of other political structures, in part from new materials and structures, for example standing armies and the civil service, and with new actors as the architects, builders and inhabitants, for example absolute monarchs, the bourgeoisie and citizens. However, the state became the political habitus of the modern citizen only after a long period of conflict, accommodation, familiarization, adaptation and modernization.

The emerging common features of this new habitus were captured in the notion of sovereignty. Particular rulers achieved dominion over a territory by various means of internal repression and external exclusion. Centralized legitimacy arose after prolonged periods of conflict, challenge and power rivalries, nearly always accompanied by resort to violence. This space called the state came to have one ruler or ruling body, one set of legitimate and legitimating rules, and a centralized bureaucracy, all to rule over a carefully defined people called citizens. This process was not uniform and is still incomplete in many parts of the world, despite largely successful efforts to export it from its home in Western Europe. The modernist narrative of convergence ignores a vast amount of difference in trajectory, calendar and content.

Tensions, gaps, contradictions, problems and challenges within states have been met with various degrees of success by maintenance activities, adaptation and change. Politics has largely been about managing maintenance and change within and between states. But for postmodernists the challenges to the state have grown and changed, both externally and internally, to a point where the structure and the inter-structural system are under excessive pressure – if not in crisis (Dunn 1994).

There are five external and six internal changes that are indicative of the challenge faced by the nation state. Externally we can start with:

(1) *Armed sovereignty.* No state can now protect its citizens successfully from determined terrorism within its borders or from external attack. Again, changes in technology have forced states to

co-operate in defence to such a point where few if any states can claim full independence or sovereignty.

(2) *Economic sovereignty*. As argued above, the world economy has been so restructured that no state can now protect and sustain itself economically from global economic forces. Transnational interpenetration has dissected states; interstate structures handling change have solidified interdependence. States can no longer perform independently even the elementary tasks of corporate intermediation between capital and labour, and between production and consumption interests, and effectiveness is seriously impaired. Capitalism has again transformed itself from a post-industrial to a postmodern basis where images and style dominate, where the logic of reproduction replaces that of production, and where post-Fordism rules.

(3) *International and transnational organizations*. These have grown and flourished in many areas. Efficacy has solidified many and legitimacy is now following to such a point that cross-cutting allegiances are fragmenting nation state legitimacy. International law has restructured the rights and duties of citizenship, allowing for new notions of political identity. Similarly, the field of social policy involves transnational agreements, structures and policies.

(4) *Decision making*. Especially in crisis, decision making is now internationalized. Problems, challenges and demands are increasingly seen as international and as therefore calling forth international solutions. This distracts citizen interests

and loyalties from the state and redirects them elsewhere.

(5) *Transnational and global cultures.* Such cultures are similarly distracting and redirecting beliefs, loyalties and orientations of citizens. Once, a natural 'imagined community' (Anderson 1991) was made up of the citizens of the nation state. Today, these communities know of no national boundaries. When placed alongside (1)–(4) above, we may begin to speak of a crisis of legitimacy for the state.

Internal changes and challenges start with:

(1) *Overload.* Modern states have few universally common functions, but one common feature has been the tendency to take on increasing roles and functions to the point where overload produces inefficiency and failure in the structure and system. Most modern states are busy jettisoning responsibilities, but with varying results and responses by citizens and producers, as Habermas (1976) and Offe (1984) predicted. The breakdown of the boundaries between public and private sectors in states is captured in the following process.

(2) *Imbrication.* Cerny (1990: 188–189) has coined the phrase to indicate the process by which the public and private sectors, structures, interests and domains become intertwined, interlocked and interpenetrated to such an extent that the ability of the state to isolate and demarcate itself is minimized.

(3) *Interest intermediation.* In the same field we have new pressures over interest intermediation. While corporatist practices have never had universal

application to all modern states, it does seem that both the corporatist players and the game have changed and that the states' capacity to successfully intermediate interest conflicts is greatly reduced. External actors have arrived and inside states consumer and consumer-oriented bodies have emerged as major league players. Dunleavy has argued, with justification, that today 'Consumption cleavages have more effect upon electoral behaviour than occupational ones' (cited in Cawson 1986: 130). Social consumption needs and desires are changing, cross-cut with market and transnational systems. Social justice is beyond consensus in a world of oscillating desires (Brittan 1977). Bargains are proving harder to make and agreements harder to sustain as old groups and interests fragment and redirect and new ones enter the game. Allegiances tend to oscillate faster with de- and realignments and increased volatility. The state has to mediate with new groups and new classes that have appeared as a concomitant to the new division of labour in the economy and in society (Lash and Urry 1987; Offe 1984, 1995). We can address these changes while looking at the following accompanying changes.

(4) *Structural changes.* Weberian bureaucracy may be exhausted as the dominant way of organizing state activities, as in a changed world it finds that its structural disadvantages outweigh its advantages. Faced with a restructuring economic, political, social and cultural world, bureaucracy seems tired if not exhausted, and is being restructured along lines indicated by the notions of decentralization, devolution, deregulation, self-management and

privatization. Centralized, unified, accountable structures of the state are in decline.

(5) *Sub-nationalisms, cultural plurality and fragmentation.* For numerous reasons the ideological and cultural bonds between the state and the citizen are loosening and being replaced by ties of a new, more various and less enduring kind. In this respect, the media's role should not be underestimated in the way they address the specific needs and interests of specific sub-groups that may not feel the same belonging as other groups.

(6) *Motivations and subjective orientations.* Subjective life-worlds and the private habitus of body and home are at the centre of the new experience of self. De-centred from tradition, the authorized and structured self seems to seek satisfaction at the level of lifestyle, consumption and a privatized style of politics, rather than in public roles and activities oriented to the state (Pekonen 1989; Reimer 1989).

In summary the traditional nation state structures, solidified over many generations, are melting around the edges and even thawing in the centre. New actors, games, fields and structures are emerging but as yet few have begun to solidify. We must now turn to the new state structures that are emerging as contenders for restructuration.

The New State

Any new state has to be able to act efficiently to accommodate the changes in its external and internal systems and worlds. It has to evolve structures to facilitate this and to create and defend spaces and roles as an actor in the new political games. To allow these to become embedded they must be effective and endure for some period. Internal and external factors are going to be bound together in a fashion that will oblige the nation state to rethink its role and structures.

In particular the state is torn between the growing efficacy and legitimacy of international and transnational structures and values, on the one side, and the fragmenting of old and reproduction of a plurality of new structures and values inside the state, on the other. The state must restructure to meet these tensions and to meet the ever-changing needs of individuals and new interests. Growth in complexity, adaptability, a capacity to read and accommodate citizens' needs as consumers, interlocking public and private worlds, de- and reregulating and commodifying services, and above all being able to facilitate a successful national capitalist economy and a successful world of private consumption and lifestyles will be central concerns.

Fragmentation and deconstruction, eclecticism and incommensurability, discontinuity and incongruity, irony and unpredictability, particularity and the lack of universalism, tolerance and ethnocentrism, prioritization of the private but the opening up of the public sphere – these are just some of the tensions, gaps and challenges facing the New State. While unlikely to collapse as quickly or precipitously as recent Eastern European political structures, state structures in Western societies must transform themselves to survive. But the ideal type of the new state characterized here will not be universal because it is not based upon the foundational and essentialist features found in models of the nation state; it will be constantly reflexive, responding to new and old actors, interests, processes and structures. A universal state structure is unlikely to emerge from the restructuring process described above; pluralism and dichotomy are likely to reign. Again, as with postmodern culture, we see the new state as containing both modern and postmodern characteristics.

To help organize our argument we will use a modified model of interest mediation taken from neo-corporatist analysis, especially from the later writing of Saunders (1985; cf. Cawson 1986: 42–44; Middlemas 1979). In this the state now mediates less between labour and capital and more obviously between consumers and producers. On the consumption side, labour interests are replaced by wider consumer interests, and on the production side, national capital interests are being replaced by transnational capital interests (Figure 7.1). What is more, the functional accommodation presumed by corporatists as its rationale is replaced by an acceptance of dysfunctional elements and asystemic tendencies in the postmodern version.

How will the new production and consumption features develop in postmodernity? First, *production*. The new state can now be characterized as having to

Figure 7.1 *Modern and postmodern corporatism*

mediate between the producer and consumer interests at the sub-national, national and international levels.

(1) Producer interests are likely to remain dominated by capitalism and in this sense the new state will be a state capitalist structure.

(2) The new state, faced with the new internal and external economy and market, will prioritize the need to mediate at all levels and between the regional, national and transnational spheres. To use Cerny's language, the state will become a 'competition state' (1990: 228–229, 241–244).

(3) Mediation between consumer and producer interests will emerge as the dominant logic and role of the state, with consumers as citizens and as the market.

(4) Imbrication and globalization will require that neither withdrawal from nor control of the market is possible.

(5) Faced with the reality of a more complex, diverse, transnational economy, the new state will play an even more difficult role than before, being prepared to intervene or withdraw, de- or reregulate, as (2) above dictates.

(6) The state will emerge as an enabling and a facilitatory enterprise as its powers for centralized control are lost.

(7) To accommodate this role the state will have to provide the legal framework to support the wider level bargaining between sub-national, national and international levels.

(8) De-centralization will become an even more attractive option to states as they try to deal with

overload problems, and especially the demands of the more self-confident expressive citizens.

Second, *consumption*. One probable feature of post-modern social and political life will be the development of what we will call 'consumer citizenship'.

(1) The new actor or citizen of the new state and of multi-state structures will demand that the state provides an environment suitable for continuous and satisfying consumption. The most pronounced feature will be that citizens centralize their interests on consumer matters rather than on modern segmental concerns of the structure, such as occupation or labour.
(2) The new consumers will focus their concerns on a number of levels and demand easy transfer and communications between them. The body, home, street, store, city, area, country, sector, the world – all of these become of more pronounced significance to them.
(3) The new politics of consumption will provide the rules of the game that the new state must play. In Britain in the 1990s the party battle has been mostly about which party has the policies most likely to allow consumption without too many risks. The growth of the service sector at the expense of others indicates the real penetration of this change in most Western economies (Mort 1989: 168–169; 1996).
(4) The state must then provide the conditions for lifestyle satisfactions for a plurality of diverse individuals and groups. Of utmost importance here is that the state recognizes that different groups not only have different interests, but that different groups also have different resources. Thus, the state must put extra efforts into making sure that groups with low levels of

capital – economic and cultural – are given the same possibilities as everyone else.

(5) Imbrication and the emergence of semi-public goods will ensure that the state is further sucked into the market.

(6) As consumer desires, needs and interests are so volatile, the new state must try to become more responsive and flexible.

(7) In the emerging consumption and lifestyle politics, the creation and expression of difference is paramount, forcing the fragmentation of old and the creation of new distinctions which will be more fragmentary, fleeting and floating, harder to read and to respond to. Political actors will inhabit a political free market and need to respond like entrepreneurs. The state will then need to marketize itself and its services to survive and to therefore 'customize' and 'commodify' itself, while the service sector will revitalize itself using the language of de-commodification (Cerny 1990: 230).

(8) In modernity much of social as against private consumption was centred on the welfare state and usually within local government. This arrangement, and with it the dual state, will continue to encounter stresses and restructurings. If the welfare state is to survive, it will have to restructure along several lines to meet the needs of the new consumer and the new economy – without forgetting to take care of those who little occupy the role of consumer: the elderly and the disabled, for instance. Problem setting and solving upon grounds of real, objective and expert needs are now cross-cut with those set by the more subjective agendas of desires and wants. If it cannot respond by learning from and by co-operating with the other welfare

sectors, the welfare state will become increasingly irrelevant, or be replaced by what Cerny calls the 'competition state' (1990: 229–230, 243–245). Duality will therefore be more complicated, redefined and restructured.

(9) In these processes civil relations and civil society will recover much ground lost to the state and become, alongside the state, a major arena for the new politics.

Problematic relations between consumption and production, and in particular between the needs to maintain and advance both production and legitimacy, will remain but in different forms, as crisis theory predicts (Jessop 1982: 106–112; O'Connor 1973). Crisis may continue to be averted but never be overcome, and then only if the state can manage to enable individuals and groups to realize their goals and to act in their achievement. The new state must ensure the right blend of production and consumption outcomes in cultural, political and economic terms; it must create the right environment if it is to retain legitimacy through time. It will have little place or time for war and must settle interest intermediation by other means.

Characteristics of the New State

We may now compare the new and old states directly using a simple model that uses the characterizations above (Table 7.1). Paradoxically perhaps, as postmodernists generally suspect binary constructions, this model helps understand the politics of postmodernity, though few of the binaries are comparative opposites but indicate partial shifts.

Table 7.1 *The old and the new state*

Old state	New state
Sovereign	Not exclusively sovereign
Territorial	Not exclusively territorial
Military	Non-military
Single rule	Shared overlapping rule
Single law	Shared overlapping law
Exclusive citizenship	Shared citizenship
National	Milti-cultural
Centralized	Devolved
Bureaucratic	Non-bureaucratic
Unitary	Non-unitary
Policy autonomy	Shared policy
Taxation and fiscal autonomy	Shared taxation and fiscal control
Welfare autonomy	Transnational welfare

In summary the new states will increasingly come to share sovereign control over their territory and citizenry with other structures and actors. They will share rules, armies, nationalities, policy making and taxation with others. Political movements may now be seen as the major vehicles and structures for carrying the consumer, lifestyle and imbricated public/private values to the new state and the appropriate vehicles for the state to involve and bargain with in the neo-corporatist system. Civil society and the state will offer new spaces for both private and public activity amongst these and other old and new structures. New politics is both called for by the new political order and acts as a stimulus to the operation and structuration occasioned by new values, beliefs and orientations. Politics has moved into areas formerly seen as private, such as feminism and sexuality, and moved out of others, leaving them to the market or civil society. Parties are sharing the public space with new groupings such as social movements.

The new politics centre upon consumer and lifestyle issues. With the citizen being replaced by the consumer, the old corporatist politics and labour politics will increasingly become anachronistic. Old allegiances and alliances will melt (left/right, radical/conservative) and new ones will form (information-rich/information-poor, north/south, workless/work-rich, married/single parents). Old issues disappear and new ones arise, creating new opportunities as well as constraints and problems. The new state and governance will have to accommodate and legitimate these changes. It will then have to negotiate accommodations on a transnational and international basis, developing the capacity for a 'cosmopolitan democracy' (Held 1995a, 1995b; Giddens 1998, 129–147).

8

Postmodern Political Futures

Within the discourses of modern political science, the making of predictions, let alone prophecies, is frowned upon as an unlikely source of benefit. There are sound arguments to advise against writing a chapter such as this. The first is philosophical, and claims that the future is epistemologically unknowable; we cannot have experience of a world that is not yet, and that has not been there to experience. The second is scientific and Humean. It claims that we cannot be sure that relations that held in the past and present will continue into the future. Prediction, like prophecy, involves an unjustifiable attempt to jump the inductive gap between evidence and inference.

A third argument against predicting the future is the wearied outcome of the long and failed dreams of various Western traditions to seek certainty, control and social engineering via the acquisition of some universal, unchanging foundational source of knowledge that would pertain into the future. Such seeds of hope have so far proved fruitless within the traditions of Western Christianity, Baconian rationalist faith in the New Atlantis, Enlightenment faith in progress, and positivism's hopes for social progress. Finally, intellectuals, especially historians and sociologists, have reflected to the point of despair on the human condition and the failure of humankind to fashion its redemption even with expanded knowledge of the past and present. The critique of eschatologies, ideologies, emancipatory totalitarian regimes, redemptive cults and charismatic leaders has echoed contemporary Western public cynicism of utopia and its preferences for dystopia.

But although we cannot know the future, we cannot take it out of the equation of politics or of human existence, and it must be entertained and studied. The reason for this is that it lies at the core of human experience, existence and being. We cannot avoid having conceptions of the future in the present. We experience uncertainty, because the world of experience is always incomplete, an unstable mixing of ideas of past, present and future. Being in the world involves the constant deconstruction of present certainty, of what is here and now, by changing knowledges of what was here and then (the past) and by beliefs about what could be, should be and will be there and then (the future). In short we live in a world of time and space where the has been, the is, and the will be coexist in present experience, albeit in a constant state of flux and tension. Who we are, what we are, what we should do, how we should live, are constructed from resources from the past and present but projected into the future, as ideas of what we want to be or do.

The Past, the Present and the Future

Each individual is inculcated into the world through inheriting narratives of the past; he or she then lives according to these narratives and any others constructed during the life-course. But what you have been and are is never enough; the present is forever consumed and annihilated in time and the issue of what will be can never be eradicated from experience. That the future cannot be guaranteed forces us to confront the possibility of loss and gain; a fear of death and nothingness, on one side, and the hope of salvation and self-affirmation, on the other (Oakeshott 1933: 303–306).

In existential and phenomenological terms, human activity is seen as the attempt to handle this condition of tension and flux. We all carry in our minds shared narratives, notions of what we were and are, but also what we could and should become. The only way to ensure success in becoming what you want to be and to avoid what you don't want is to act in the present. Private activity is much about self-maintenance and change made necessary and possible by time and by the knowledge that there is a future. Public activities such as politics are premised on the same necessities but are directed to collective maintenance, survival and change. Politics, as Oakeshott, Voegelin, Arendt, Heidegger and Wolin see it, is essentially about the maintenance and change of public identity in the context of time and space, and concerns about the future; an insight born into the modern world in the work of Niccolò Machiavelli (Anglo 1969; Orr 1973; Pocock 1973, 1975).

For Machiavelli time was a cruel mistress who left too much to the play of chance and fortune. The workings of Fortuna, the goddess of chance, were a paradigm for the political leader or Prince. Politics was trepidatious enough when princes were faced with their own limited power, others seeking *gloria* and success, and their own lack of competence or *virtù*, but the double jeopardy came with the uncertainty and fickleness of Fortuna to ensure a successful future. Lacking knowledge of the future but seeking the fulfilment of ambition, a politician is obliged to do all he can to limit the chances of failure. The most important quality to gain and keep is practical political skills or *virtù*, to ensure your enemies are outwitted and your allies are prepared. But Fortuna, being a woman, is capable of making a mockery of the plans of even the most virtuous and ruthless ruler, her fickleness being notorious. Yet even she can be outguessed on occasions by the virtuous; we can anticipate and build defences against her capricious behaviour as the Florentines built dikes against the floods, we can improve our anticipation by studying her past so as to calculate her more predictable wiles, and we can be sure that fortune will favour the young and the bold.

From Machiavelli, political science may learn that although we can never know or predict the future with certainty, we can never and must never cease from the engagement of trying to understand the future from the vantage point of the past and the present. The future is unavoidably at the centre of human existence, the rationale of practical politics and a cause for the concern of political scientists. But not only are conceptions of the future unavoidable and necessary; our constructions and understandings of the future often shape and determine activity.

The position of politicians and political scientists on the future are different but related. Western democratic politicians have always sought to win power by shaping the future; elections may be won or lost on the issue of which party has the most compelling vision of what will be. Promises of entry into heaven, heaven on earth, a nation state, a thousand-year Reich, communist autonomy, increased wealth or welfare have vied with each other for public support and analytic scrutiny.

Politicians want to know how electorates or other consumers of their policies will respond to their initiatives. They seek to build dikes against the ravages of ill fortune as well as increasing their own power and virtue.

Political scientists rightly study these phenomena, but, having learned from the lessons above, avoid flirting with the future themselves (Oakeshott 1933: 311–315). A few exceptions may be noted. Many political historians have extrapolated from past to future, foreseeing the decline of old orders, cultures, ideologies and parties and the rise of others; much of the business of psephology has been harnessed in recent years, with variable success, to predicting the outcomes of elections, referenda and policies. Futurology is a fast-expanding study of alternative futures, and has at least one journal to espouse its cause. Three schools can be identified: the *positivists*, who seek a science of the future built around new scientific methods and statistics providing reliable prediction; the *forecasters*, who work by extrapolating from past behaviour to future outcomes; and the *conjecturists*, who revel in intellectual speculation on the possibility of new world orders. John Stuart Mill, Marx, Durkheim and Mannheim are examples of the positivists; Daniel Bell, Ronald Inglehart and the UK-based Henley Centre illustrate the forecasters; and Jürgen Habermas, Alvin Toffler, Anthony Giddens and Ulrich Beck are good examples of the conjecturists. We shall explore the future from within the conjecturist camp.

Exploring the Future

In what follows we are going to refer to the future as the imagined human world that may come given certain articulations, a personal or shared world of ideas, practices and institutions. This world of ideas exists in the present but is currently a 'construction', 'visualization' or 'projection' from the present into the world to come, the not yet. In this sense the future is not some metaphysical entity – another dimension to the present like the 'after life' – but a feature and dimension of everyday present consciousness and experience. In academic terms we can reflect upon this as do philosophers of time; we can study cases of its formation as with study of visionary art and literary utopias; we can look at the way advertisers and politicians use constructions of the future to affect present behaviour; we can sociologize on the social factors accompanying the emergence of utopianisms, eschatologies and other futures; and in political science we can study the methodologies for prediction and theoretical and ideological formations of the future.

We cannot know or predict the future, but what we can do, in addition to the above, is to work out the implications of the range of futures that are being suggested in postmodern thinking, culture and practices. We can elaborate the range of futures generated and then elucidate their implications for understanding political change. We take the diagnosis of the past and present outlined in earlier chapters and add our prognosis.

This brings us to the topic of values discussed in Chapter 6. All visions of the future are a complex mix of not only understandings of the facts of past and present but also evaluations of these and valuations of what we prefer, wish for, want, need, desire, expect, and think we ought, must and should have in the future. Values and ideals are as much facts of our consciousness and our visions of past and future as are all other types of facts, and moral facts play as much role in determining our actions as any others (Grote 1870: 145–147; Oakeshott 1933: 283–285, 307–11). Behaviour is shaped by ideals: we feel we ought to preserve the environment, save whales, and treat people of different genders, sexualities, races and colours equally. Ideals of what ought to be in the future will affect behaviour just as much as the facts that a person lives in the country, fishes for a living, and is a woman, lesbian and an African. Our ideas about what it is to be an African are a mixture of types of facts, and some of these are moral facts about how an African ought to behave in a certain situation. As Winch, Searle and Foot argue, moral beliefs, rules and principles, for example the rule that one ought to wash one's hands before cooking, determine actions as much as scientific beliefs about hygiene and health (Foot 1967: 83–100; Searle 1967: 101–114; Winch 1974: 78–111).

Postmodernism's attitude to the future is complex. First, postmodernism is concerned with futures, not the future; there is never one future, but a plurality of diverse futures present at any one time in the minds of individuals and groups. Next, a postmodern view does not entail one linear or unilinear progression to the future. The move from modern to postmodern is not a case of unilinear and universal change, nor a new grand narrative, but an eclectic mixing of old and new elements in a variety of distinct local and global forms. Postmodernity will have not a future but a variety of futures.

Furthermore, postmodernists are focused on the notion of reflexivity, not determinism, so the variety of futures posited is understood as the outcome not only of global and local forces, but also of the intended actions of expressive individuals and groups. Increasingly, the world of management, counselling and life training is devoted to participants' visualizations of a positive future, or goals that they can realize in practice. Indeed, with this rediscovery of persons as agents, local futures may be more responsive to the intended plans and actions of agents than was ever envisaged in the medieval and feudal worlds.

Locality and difference also characterize postmodern political futures. It is likely that particular futures moulded to specific environments will multiply; and not as subcultures to the dominant but as a feature of the dominant. Local and regional political solutions will differ around leadership, organization, agenda and support. So postmodern futures will also be plural and pluralized rather than singular and monolithic, both because central leaders have lost the capacity and will to impose centralized solutions, and because their former customers have changed products and allegiances. The bricolaged nature of political spaces is likely to become the dominant pattern in Western societies. Alongside this, we expect that various futures will be shared in other places and cultures in the world. Globalization will ensure that transnational and international futures will be forged at all levels, and especially across sub-governmental levels.

We may now look at the major constructions of the future in recent social and political theory and try to identify their key features. The dominant conjectures can be typified as the *critical*, the *pessimistic* and the *optimistic*. In what follows we identify with the optimists. As noted in Chapter 1, Rosenau (1992: 138–154) defined two categories in regard to political futures: sceptics and affirmatives. The former constructs 'the world as inevitably moving toward a final collapse, oblivion and self-destruction that cannot be postponed' (1992: 139). The key examples are nihilistic in orientation, not advancing change but simply advocating withdrawal, ironic detachment and deconstruction of the conventional and democratic in politics. Rosenau's affirmatives conjecture

> a range of new political movements organized around everything from peace, ecology/environment, feminism, green politics, nationalism, populism, and anarchism to 'spiritual fitness disciplines', parapsychology, psychokinesis, and New Age Movements. They encompass 'communities of resistance', poor people's movements and therapy groups. They bring together the oppressed, mentally ill, citizens with disabilities, the homeless, and generally disadvantaged. (1992: 144)

For us, this binary is too categorical, too restrictive, excluding pessimists who are not nihilists and optimists who operate with conventional political activities above the level of subcultures and social movements. The categories should be able to embrace a very broad and deep mass of political cultures, behaviours, practices, institutions and processes, including old as well as new political forms – central and local, national and global, formal and informal, democratic and non-democratic. Postmodern political futures we consider to involve the whole range of existing and additional matters and not just a narrow range of alternatives. But first we must explain why we eschew the argument of the crisis theorists and pessimists.

Critical postmodern futures entertain the idea that modern politics is in a terminal state; some point of no return has been reached, leading eventually to the demise of the old and the unlikelihood of anything substantial taking its place. Such views are contained in the 'crisis' literature of recent years, especially by Habermas (1976), Offe (1984, 1985) and O'Connor (1973, 1984), as well as in the nihilistic literature of Lyotard (1984), Vattimo (1988, 1992), Virilio (1990), Baudrillard (1984), Kroker and Cook (1988) and Edelman (1988).

The problem with this theory is not so much its lack of internal coherence but that it fails to resonate with the expressed feelings, needs and desires of citizens in Western democracies, and that it does not seem to find an echo in their political behaviour. The theory is contradicted in the findings of the 'Beliefs in Government' project that studied crisis tendencies through changes in public attitudes to democratic systems in thirteen Western countries since the Second World War (Borre and Scarbrough 1995; Kaase and Newton 1995; Klingemann and Fuchs 1995; Niedermayer and Sinnott 1995; van Deth and Scarbrough 1995). The study does not negate the argument that crisis tendencies have only been sublimated and that they will evolve towards a more complete crisis in the future, but we do not agree. Western liberal democracies living with capitalism seem to be uniquely equipped to respond to critical demands and to reinvent themselves anew when required (Kaase and Newton 1995: 17–39, 150–172; Thompson 1996: 84–103). The nihilistic prophetic mood of the sceptics has neither spread to mass populations as yet, nor have the publics exhibited the withdrawal and non-participation conjectured by them.

By pessimists we mean those critics who, while eschewing the vision of collapse, still fear the worst, having serious reservations about the capacity of liberal representative democracies to generate a type of politics that will accommodate the new demands of its publics. This position is held by many writers on post-modern politics in the West, such as structuralist postmodernists like Jameson (1989, 1991), Harvey (1989) and Smart (1993), and most of the critical analysts of post-industrialization such as Bauman (1992), Bell (1973), Heller and Feher (1989), Lyon (1994), Poster (1990) and White (1993). We will criticize the pessimistic position through an elaboration of the optimistic theory, espoused also by Connolly (1995), Crook et al. (1992), Laclau (1990), Melucci (1988, 1989), Mouffe (1988, 1992, 1993), Soper (1993), Squires (1993), Weeks (1993, 1995), Yeatman (1994), Young (1993) and Bauman (1993) in his more positive mood. While recognizing the possibility of unresolved tensions and crisis tendencies in liberal democracies we identify other positive possibilities that build upon more active citizenship; more creativity and cosmopolitan accommodation of rivalries and conflicts, a 'cosmopolitan democracy'.

The Progressive Potential of Postmodernity

Unlike Rengger, who conjectures that postmodernity will herald both 'the best and worst of times', we will argue for the optimistic potential of 'better' times. It must be made clear that what we are addressing here is the postmodern *potential*. The transformation of societies from modern to postmodern in no way necessarily leads to better societies. There are both risks and opportunities involved. But we argue that the processes typical of postmodernity may give individuals the possibilities to express themselves – individually and collectively – in ways that may force political parties, organizations and states to react to their demands. This may not happen: major obstacles are the unequal power held by different groups in society and the risk of widening gaps between information-rich and information-poor. But it is not an unlikely development given certain articulations and it is one worth outlining – if only to show what the postmodern potential may be.

The postmodern potential will be evaluated by three criteria that we may have in Western democracies: more activist citizens dealing with more responsive political bodies in more areas of life and the globe (Rengger 1995: 206). First, in this scenario, citizens in Western democracies will continue to become more discerning, expressive, value-oriented and activistic, while becoming less slavish to older allegiances to parties and states. They will hence become more like the ideal of the democratic citizen. Second, due to citizen action, organizations will have to abandon patriarchal control and respond to these new citizens and groups by becoming less opaque, more answerable, accountable and adaptable, having to reconstitute themselves regularly as citizens and their demands change, the polity becoming more like the ideal of a pluralistic democratic civil society. Third, globalization will spread these democratic processes faster around the world, penetrating even the most modernist of all environments.

We see the first criterion encapsulated in the idea that politics will continue to become more of an expressive or *performative* activity, as argued by Butler, namely that political speech and activity will not represent reality but be expressions of a certain kind of lifestyle and form of life. There is a core self or identity in, for and to women, according to Butler. The appearance of a

145

feminine identity follows performances that are learned, constructed and practised by gendered females and is not the innocent, surface representation of either an innate nature or an internalized cultural construct. Being male or female requires knowing how to act or perform. Through imitation, a system of rewards and sanctions, and our command of cultural and linguistic conventions, we learn to stylize our bodies and gestures, dress, walk and talk, and use grooming and grammar to project ourselves as women or men (Butler 1997; Seidman 1998: 270–271). But gender, like all other identities, is a performance that can be subverted, remodelled and performed anew. Just as 'drag' subverts gender, so youth cultures subvert adolescence and social movements subvert parties.

The second criterion is exemplified in the notion of group *performativity* as espoused by Yeatman and Cerny. For them, postmodern states are forced to accommodate functionally to the marketplace of demands from their internal and external environment. Performativity here means being functional, being able to be like an impressario, to maintain and generate legitimacy by entrepreneurial and inventive performances. The art of politics becomes the art of performance.

The third criterion we see encapsulated in the ideas of postmodernization, mediazation and globalization discussed by Held, Cerny and Crook et al., namely that regions and each state will have to *accommodate* the ensemble of cultures and forces that are generated in society via global penetration (Butler 1997; Cerny 1990; Crook et al. 1992; Pinkney 1997; Yeatman 1994: 110–117). This suggests the development of a 'Cosmopolitan Democracy' (Held, 1995b; Giddens 1998, 136–147).

We may summarize our conjectures while working from the internal narrative of this book. We expect the languages, typologies and theories of postmodernity to evolve in ever more convoluted yet constructive forms as the cyclical processes of linguistic change and postmodernization evolve. Although arguments about the post-postmodern are already abroad, we expect that terminologies of late modernity, reflexive modernity and postmodernity will interpenetrate while new discourses emerge.

Postmodernization, understood as the interplay of numerous processes in shaping society and polity, will ensure that the outcomes and shapes of things will continue to be less predictable and more ambiguous, more particular, local and global, and less universal, regional and national. We expect globalization to accelerate in speed and penetrate further in the future thus hastening the postmodernization process. Many areas of politics will find themselves interconnected in new ways with global bodies; institutions such as health, law and policing will become more interconnected with the transnational and global. Postmodern international relations theory, for instance, tells us that the old order is ceasing to operate functionally and that a new order is taking shape (Cooper 1996; Hoffman 1995). Here interdependence is replacing sovereignty as the logic of international politics, involving a restructuring of the modern state rather than its demise (Brown 1988; Bull and Watson 1984; Dunn 1994; Held 1995a: 96–120; 1995b; Hoffman 1995; Rengger 1989; Thompson 1996; Weber 1994). Held's notions of a cosmopolitan democracy and governance capture much of what we consider to be potential, possible and desirable (Held 1995b: 270–286; Held and Archibugi 1995). The politics of the Gulf War and the disintegration of the Soviet Union and Yugoslavia are indicative of the sort of problems to be faced and the way that postmodern politics will create particularistic – and highly ambiguous – solutions.

We also highlighted the role that the new consumer and the new consumer culture will have in determining the shape of the new state and the new international order. National and state politics as a corporate fix between key interests and pressures, especially capital and the military, will be replaced by ones in which these interests must interact with new forces and movements with their own vocabularies, values and modes of operation. Recent conflicts over the disposal of effluents, chemicals and radioactive waste, and the decommissioning of oil rigs in the North Sea, indicate the sort of open and more pluralized types of international politics we expect here. At the heart of this we expect the ethicization of international, transnational and global politics, as the penetration of green and feminist politics illustrates. Relating the two is the idea that international politics will be about maintaining and enhancing the lifestyles of individuals and groups and not of states and capital. Having created the global consumer and empowering him or her to create a personalized lifestyle, the state and capital will find that they have created a rod for their own backs, a burden that they must carry or face delegitimation, as the politics of baby milk, the international arms industry and animal experimentation testify.

The future direction of politics will remain unclear, and that will continue to evoke uncertainty, but unpredictability produces a feeling that actors and actions count and that activist practical politics is worth pursuing. Furthermore, the mass media open up the world to practically everybody. Knowledge is no longer restricted to the powerful. Thus, individuals know more than before about alternative ways of living. They get visions of other kinds of lives, forcing political bodies to continue the process towards the new politics and towards a greater individualization and pluralization of politics.

Expressivist selves, we conjecture, will emerge as the dominant form in the postmodern future; selves dedicated to the endless task of reinventing themselves in line with the new cultural forces in their environment. We expect citizens to be more confident about their capacity to act for themselves and to negotiate solutions to their own problems. We expect them to join less but do more. While in extreme forms this may threaten the like capacity of other individuals and groups to create their own solutions, we anticipate that with the appropriate kind of civil law, policing, education and social policy, the prediction of social anarchy and crisis will not be realized. Autonomy in decision making will also spread among groups who we argue will be able to create, maintain and adapt a kaleidoscope of alternative lifestyles. We do not anticipate that disembedded individuals and groups will withdraw into nihilism; instead they will gravitate out into more heterogeneous and customized life-worlds.

Problems of inequality will remain but will take new shapes as the old lines of stratification are permeated and new lines emerge. Those located higher in social space will have advantages over those placed lower; possession of both economic and cultural capital will continue to affect both power and expressive ability. But in postmodernity, the most excluded will have more sources and resources for resistance, self-affirmation and self-realization than in modernity. They will be able to form new allegiances, partake in more networks, thereby empowering themselves.

Postmodern patterns of values, in which there is no hierarchy, grounding norms or essentials – except the belief that everyone should be able to order their values as they wish so long as this is compatible with everybody else being able to do the same – will spread. We expect that the individualization of value patterns and lifestyles will flourish to the point where bricolage may be a restrictive concept. But we conjecture that whereas traditional loyalties may diminish, we may expect a newer and deeper attachment to the newer personalized patterns which will trump dissonance. Although we may reasonably expect less predictability and more complexity, rather than breakdown or withdrawal as a result, we expect new attachments and loyalties. Political behaviour, we conjecture, will be less routinized and conventional. We expect more expressive direct action and unconventional forms and types of activity. Political parties will continue to decline in size and significance and will have to restructure permanently to maintain electoral support and democratic legitimacy.

New politics, especially around new social movements, will spread and become established as the norm in Western societies. New issues will continue to arise incessantly as long as repressed minorities move beyond resistance to advocacy. Social units will not only be pluralized by globalization but will become internally culturally plural. Multi-culturalism will become more of a reality at the same time as the world becomes more cosmopolitan. We expect the demands and pressures on governments, states and international bodies to mount inexorably but without too much fear of overload so long as they follow the policy of downloading rights and responsibility to citizens and groups. More difficult is the process of postmodern law making and adjudication.

In response to the problem of governance in postmodern society, we expect, first, the sovereign nation state to have to give way to the pluralized form of civil society, where government holds the ring between interweaving social and political groupings (Hall 1995; Tester 1992; Giddens 1998, 69–89). As Kleinig (1996) speculates, the only practical and credible form of policing in a postmodern world is some form of social peacekeeping (see also Gibbins 1998a). Governance will be less about enterprise activity and more about facilitating and imposing a meaningful narrative on unusual results.

Second, we expect that legislating for society will have to return to a more open, public and unpredictable form of politics than traditional parliamentary and presidential forms of politics have encouraged or allowed. The Athenian notion of politics, as the public activity of free persons negotiating how they wish to live, could turn out to be the most functional, effective and legitimate mode of government in the postmodern world. Ideal pure democratic politics allows individuals and groups to express themselves, allows government to download decisions it cannot make without excluding groups, and allows a genuine multicultural politics to flourish. This needs to be attached to a new form of democracy, which, as most commentators suggest, should transcend and add to the failed politics of representation (Bobbio 1987, 1997; Yturbe

1997: 377–400). We expect that pressure from citizens and groups will forge new democratic accommodations to make good the present democratic deficit, with such options as people's panels, referenda and polling. Direct democracy, as it is called, will help here by allowing interested citizens to help shape public policy between elections using the new technologies (Budge 1996).

For democracy to flourish it must respond to the political agenda of everyday life, of workplace, home and sexuality, and we expect politics to spread down to these sites. Democracy will exist without a dominant interest or ideology and should set about the agonistic task of trying to create policy out of continuous dialogue. Agonistic and dialogical democracy, we conjecture, will flourish in a postmodern age. Agonism refers to the situation posed by Isaiah Berlin, William Connolly and John Grote, in which we accept that there is no a priori or definable system of priority between moral principles and goals in a democracy, no solution to identity/difference posed by pluralism and multi-culturalism; a situation that consequently forces citizens and governments to make agonizing choices between policy goals and to prioritize for themselves (Berlin 1969: 167–172; Connolly 1991: 178–179, 191–193; 1995; Gray 1996: 66; 1997: 35–50; Grote 1876: xiv–xv). By a dialogical democracy we mean one in which procedural factors and wealth play a secondary role to conversation, argument and debate in settling agonistic decisions and conflicts. Again this returns us to the potential within postmodernity for a more Athenian practice of politics, but one in which the small *agora* or spatial marketplace is replaced by the global *agora*, the global marketplace of ideas, knowledge, media and messages. It also makes us reconsider the formal and procedural structures that would support such a dialogical and agonistic democracy (Crouch and Marquand 1995).

Our answer to this challenge is civil society and the idea of government as holding the ring and facilitating the debate and governance as social peacekeeping between contestants, some of whom will see rule keeping as a restraint on their communitarian enterprise goal-oriented mission. How can one speak about social justice as a universal in a society, let alone achieve social justice, when most people speak the vocabularies of the groups to which they belong? How, when identity formation involves assimilation with some particular others and distinguishing oneself from the rest, can one find a shared vocabulary, narrative and values (Squires 1993: 7–12)? How do we get a sense of something shared when difference is the logic and practice of membership? Much of recent political theory, and practical activist politics today, is devoted to solving this conundrum in its various guises, but especially the debate between libertarians, pluralists and communitarians over identity, difference, plurality and multi-culturalism. The success of the postmodern conjecture may well hang on a successful outcome of such negotiations (Beiner 1995; Bellamy 1992: 252–261; Connolly 1995; Kymlicka 1995, 1997; Miller 1995; Oldfield 1990; Parekh 1997; Rawls 1993; Walzer 1983; Young 1990).

Postmodernist theory and practice offer a myriad of solutions to these problems. One is to accept the demands of membership but to recognize that living involves membership of many different yet overlapping groups, say one's family, church, profession and friendship network. No relation and network can trump all others, and indeed our identities are precisely the blended and constructed accommodations we reach between them. All identities, even in strong communities, are themselves accommodations from previous blending processes. A second postmodern insight is that identity means and involves the maintenance of sameness despite change, continuity of features through time. Our changing looks through the life cycle illustrate this, as do our changing personalities and moral preferences. Time ensures we cannot keep everything as it was and is. We have to rebuild, structure and reinvent ourselves ever anew. Paradoxically, holding onto an allegiance or solidarity is still accommodating and changing it, and so engaging in its change. Reactionary rhetoric is usually a cover for a radical renewal.

Next, postmodernists can offer the old insight that pluralism and liberalism allow more individuals and groups to renew their identities than do authoritarian regimes. The politics of exclusion and repression can satisfy but one group – and even that doubtfully – while a postmodern governance that encourages tolerance can satisfy most if not all. As we argued in Chapter 6, the commonality in a postmodern polity can be based on second-order agreement on a civil order vocabulary and rules, leaving groups to operate on whatever first-order moral principles and beliefs they wish. Many offers exist for this vocabulary and its rules, but we propose that the following constitutive principles for a postmodern civil society may form part of what is needed.

Principles for a Postmodern Civil Society

In postmodern times ethical and civil rules and principles are not so much discovered as made; they are to be considered as contingent artefacts and not as a priori principles. In Parekh's terms, we need a set 'of moral and political principles that are both universally valid and capable of accommodating cultural diversity and autonomy' (1993: 173). In our terms, what principles would all members of a multi-cultural society or cosmopolis require if each and all were to maximize their authenticity and expressive potential?

(1) *The equity principle* requires that like cases be treated alike and unlike cases differently, depending upon some agreement upon what are morally significant features. The similar demands of groups, for example for places to worship or rave in, are equally respected; and the right to be different in their type and form of worship or rave is also equally respected. The morally significant dimensions of cases can be debated in a shared political space so as to create the universal civil rules of incorporation of any group. So there should be rules about joining and leaving; entitlements and obligations; adjudication and punishment. Hard cases would have to be agreed upon and these agonistic decisions would leave some groups upset. Hence a group who wanted compulsory clitoridectomy or castration as a condition of membership may have to be disappointed.

On what postmodern grounds can one justify this? (2) *The principle of revocability* argues that no individual or group should create or invoke any contract that does not leave its members capable of revoking membership of any grouping and of entering into and enjoying the benefits of membership of another grouping or relationship, community or agreement. This principle is justified by the overriding postmodern concern that individuals should be able to join and leave relationships when and how they wish throughout their lives. A group that imposed bodily mutilation would be prohibited on the grounds that members would lose their freedom to revoke membership and join another relationship with different rules of association.

How can we deal with traditions of intergroup distrust? (3) *The toleration principle* demands that while no group can be expected to accept, agree with or support the beliefs and practices of others, they should tolerate their right to practise in exchange for reciprocal tolerance. By toleration here we mean putting up with something whether we like it or not; it is a necessary evil based upon expediency.

Do we need a stronger version of toleration grounded in an autonomy, neutrality or impartiality principle to meet our needs for a commonly accepted civil language, ethic and set of civil rules to operate? Must we urge upon governments the respect for people's autonomy or the duty of neutrality or impartiality? Like Mendus we believe autonomy, neutrality and impartiality to be universalistic principles that cannot 'guarantee a society which is truly diverse and tolerant' (1989: 145). Autonomy is rejected in many forms of life where immersion in the group is the aim, and postmodernists cannot abide the theory as they accept an identity that is derived and constructed from diverse social, not personal, sources (Theile 1997: 83–85). Neutrality, like impartiality, fails because it controverts the notion of belonging, is explicitly rejected in the rules of membership of many groups who demand commitment, and because in postmodern theory it is impossible; we all come from somewhere when we reason and act. Similar arguments can be marshalled against the addition of an impartiality principle (Mendus 1996). These objections are valid if by impartiality we mean a demand that we never show preferential treatment to particular groups or individuals, for it is clear that in most cases, as with parenthood, we must do precisely this (Walzer 1997: 87–89).

However, we could add (4) an *impartiality clause* if we understand it to mean a refusal to show undue and unjustified partiality in the exercise of a role where it is not appropriate. We are required to be partial in every walk of life, even in adjudicating the law; what we can and should avoid in a postmodern society is undue and unwarranted preferential treatment. So we expect the police to be partial in the exercise of the law in cases of defending victims, but we do not expect them to favour victims' cases that mirror their own cultural preferences or identities in the practice of policing. In a postmodern polity the police should be impartial in the singular sense of not being unduly diligent in assisting the interests, values and good of any particular group in society.

Who is obliged and who pays to support the polity? (5) *The stakeholding principle* is that all those with a stake in the outcomes of the civil society should be entitled to shape it and benefit from it, and equally they should be obliged to obey its rules and provide financial support via taxation.

How do we deal with spaces that rival groups claim as their own? (6) *The shared space principle* states that no group should be able to monopolize spaces that have significance to many groups, for example footpaths, the skies and, for that matter, the Internet.

Why? (7) *The public goods principle* states that no public goods (goods that cannot be owned privately and are preconditions for the benefit of all groups, for example water, air, roads, health) should be monopolized or damaged by any one group but be maintained and enhanced by and at the cost of all benefiting individuals and groups. These principles we offer as a voice in the conversation that will shape the postmodern polity. We conjecture they would provide a second-order common moral order that would sustain a civil association and polity.

Political leadership in such a society would have to take on a new shape and role. Centralized bureaucratic leadership we see as the most threatened of all modern achievements as trust seems to seep away from it as knowledge grows. But the task of restoring trust to leaders is made easier as we expect fewer policies and decisions from leaders and a greater capacity to tell stories and narratives we like. Bound to the media, postmodern politicians can and will fashion the personal politics of charisma in ever new inventive ways (Pekonen 1989). The complexity of leadership, we anticipate, will pose problems never encountered by modern politicians and will force us into a politics of experts, advisers and presentation experts ever committed to putting the best spin on any situation and decision. The art and form of governance we also expect to change in a direction indicated by Fox and Miller (1995) and Rhodes (1996: 652–667); a direction the former identifies with postmodernity (cf. Rosenau and Czempiel 1992).

Governance, as increasingly pluralized, now amounts to 'self-organizing networks', who are willingly or necessarily involved in 'publicly interested discourses which transcend hierarchical institutions', and which, because it recognizes the competence and knowledge of many citizens, allows them to operate without government intrusion (Loader, 1997; Rhodes 1996: 666–667). In the postmodernized public administration we expect that power and responsibility will devolve down to groups, and outwards to transnational bodies. We expect that new technologies will remove the necessity for centralized mass Fordist styles and forms of management and so lead to the decentralization of public administration. Again the civil service culture should expect to be transformed as the culture in which it has been embedded melts and new cultural forces enter. As a consequence of the feminization of the civil service, the process for policy critique, formation and implementation will become less routinized and rational. The fuzzy logic of new technology will impact upon public management as 'what works here and now' replaces the practice of 'what worked there and then'. Plurality, difference, eclecticism, complexity and flexibility will mark the new public administration.

Finally, we conjecture that postmodern politics will necessitate a new kind of citizenship and social policy so as to include all that had escaped modernist politics. The new citizenship and social policy will be premised upon the capacity of governments to provide the conditions for effective membership for all. To do this we must move beyond the liberal theoretical agenda of rights and move to one of enablement. For some, postmodernization leads to the fragmentation of welfare, for others to its end, but there will remain the need, the desire and the political imperative for membership and loyalty, solidarity and belonging at some level, and social policy will provide the formal and informal structure for this (Carter 1998; Hirst and Khilnani 1996; Leonard 1997).

The levels at which membership and solidarity will gel are debatable, but we consider they will ebb away from the nation state down to smaller and more transient communities and upwards and out towards transnational and international groupings.

We consider that welfare provision will have to be redirected and restructured towards the tasks of enabling a plurality of potentially incommensurable individuals and groups to realize their narratives and lifestyles. Imposition of a modernist agenda of fashioning a new citizen, as with the founding fathers of the modern welfare state, Beveridge, Marshall and Titmus, will have to give way to a more pluralistic, personal and lifestyle-oriented – and facilitatory – agenda and model (Gibbins 1998a). In this individuals and groups will play a greater role in defining their needs and constructing personalized solutions. The state will interact with friendship groups, voluntary associations, social movements and international bodies to perm welfare packages. But for many, negotiating their way through the new order will be problematic without the access to the new knowledge, discourses and media necessary for success. Inclusion will mean a redirection of state efforts and not their diminution if we are to create an information democracy via community informatics (Everard 1998; Loader 1997, 1998; Tsagarousianou et al. 1997).

We will summarize these conjectures by looking at

the assertion that for politics the fates of postmodernity and new politics are closely aligned. Postmodernization is creating a new political agenda which includes gender, sexuality, the environment, animals, child care, sport, the body, identity, the self and the media. Many items on the agenda are single issues and may have a short shelf life; most will involve ethical and value issues at their heart; most will activize new actors and make decision making more complex; all will involve the imbrication of public and private spheres (Weintraub and Kumar 1997). This means that politics will be located in different sites and spaces, such as the everyday sites of city centres, shopping malls, ports, bedrooms and kitchens, television programmes such as soap operas and talk shows, and one's body (Mort 1989, 1996; Shields 1992; Squires 1994). All will make inclusion, direct representation, self-construction and communicative ethics more central (Benhabib 1992; Seitz 1995). Political parties, we conjecture, will find legitimacy, trust and support harder to acquire and loyalty harder to maintain (Misztal 1996)

Faced with complexity, parties, we envisage, will reinvent themselves at regular intervals, as have the New Democrats under Clinton and New Labour under Blair. Both repositioned their party above the old party and class divisions. Both sought a 'third way' in policy and ideology terms, rejecting the binaries of left and right while in fact perming policies from parties at home and abroad (Bobbio 1996; Giddens 1994, 1998). Changing the vocabulary of politics was the key indicator of the enterprise and one that probably had the biggest effect. Distancing themselves from the past, these two postmodern impresarios sought to reposition their parties and themselves, to claim to be at the 'radical centre' yet doing nothing that would detract from the inculcation of a feelgood factor. Both sought to rise above the politics of interest; they sought to bring in excluded groups and to respond to public feelings identified through a process of opinion polling and panel testing. The re-invention of old ways and the invention of new ways, we see as the likely form of future politics.

The challenges to governance we see as changing, and the most immediate, we conjecture, are multi-culturalism inside societies and risk management between them (Beck 1992, 1996; Kymlicka 1995). What is now being called the 'politics of difference', which involves old and new groupings using politics as a form of identity formation and realization, poses all decision-making bodies with seemingly irreconcilable pressures. A postmodern multi-cultural and pluralistic politics as espoused by Parekh, Miller and others seems the construction most likely to bear the burden of difference, whereas the Beck and Giddens alliance seems to indicate the new direction in risk management (Beck 1997; Giddens 1997; Haber 1994; Miller 1995; Parekh 1993, 1997).

This is not to detract from the importance of 'statecraft' and 'selfcraft' in lifestyle politics, a core issue in postmodern politics (Digeser 1995; Seglow 1996: 42–45). To allow self-management of the transformation required we may still need a kind of therapeutic politics as well as information politics; politics in which politicians mirror therapists, offering narratives of past, present and future that make some sense of dissonance in difficult times. In postmodern new politics, not only is there a new style, but style as such becomes essential. Anne Phillips (1993, 1995) has defined one such possible new style, a kind of 'politics of presence' that includes formerly excluded groups and that can coexist with a deliberative democracy. The 'dialogical', 'discursive' and 'agonistic' styles already discussed also offer glimpses of possible futures, as do the demands by Habermas and others for 'deliberative rights' which will accommodate openness, access, participation, authorship, reflexivity and conflict mediation (Blaug 1996: 71–77). Current and highly contested debates on the future of democracy suggest lines for postmodernists to explore (Held 1993; Touraine 1997).

As important to the politics of difference we consider the politics of solidarity and re-engagement. Reinventing old solidarities, inventing new ones and forging and then maintaining a re-engagement of all publics with the civic order will be the hardest and most crucial job of governance (Beck 1996; Callan 1997; Hirst and Khilnani 1996; Squires 1993). Non-participatory and non-representational styles of direct democratic politics such as those explored by Botwinick (1993) and Budge (1996) may flourish as may the demand for more 'people's panels'. Political aesthetics, we consider, will, like values, play a role so long relegated by utilitarian political demands; how it seems will be as important as how it is. But all of these are compatible with the idea that the new politics will accompany a new and enlarged role for politics.

Politics as envisaged in the classical republican tradition – as the public activity of reconciling conflicts over identity and policy between free citizens in a shared space – will resurrect as well as be reinvented following the lines indicated by Arendt and Oakeshott (Dagger 1997; d'Entreve 1994; Hirst 1994; Miller 1995; Sandel 1996; Pettit 1997). Neo-republicanism is a name we may coin for this direction in theory and practice, and may run alongside the prediction that the global order may look once again like the renaissance alliances of city states envisaged by Rorty, and pursued by the Catalan leader Jordi Pugol in his aim to unite Barcelona with Toulouse and Milan to effect a triangle of influence that cuts across national and state boundaries. Some authors consider universal solidarity to be a product of local and particular accommodations while others consider that as the lines of difference are fabrications of history, so are their erasure (Phillips 1994: 251–252). For new social movement theorists such as Melucci and Touraine, by pluralizing and articulating difference we cross-cut and diminish the lines of class conflict that have dominated modern politics (Gladwin 1994: 62–64; Lacey and Frazer 1994: 80). We agree that the best chance of new solidarity in postmodernity lies not in shoring up old lines of identity, such as class, nation and religion – a politics of reaction – but in engaging in the new politics of diversity and difference. Without the fixed battle lines that class, nation and religion provide, conflicts diminish or are transformed into less fractious contests. But we agree with Sandel (1996) that the new republicanism must avoid the defects of American liberal proceduralist republicanism and allow more direct, effective and continuous participation by citizens.

We come back finally to the mood or general prognosis of postmodernity. If we ignore the crisis theorists, as we argued we should, we are left with the choice we posed between pessimists and optimists. We have here favoured an optimistic mood by personal attachment and analytic force. Zygmunt Bauman's pessimism arises from the inability of postmodern projects to solve the problems of inequality and others found in modernity, and in the understanding that 'the messiness of the human predicament is here to stay' (1993: 245; 1997). For us, optimism arises from the opportunities offered by the processes of postmodernity, by individual action, and by the articulation between these factors, as well as by the liberation that post-utopian thought provides. Postmodernists do not have to entertain the ironic mood, whether detached or engaged, that Rorty evokes as necessary if we are to traverse the postmodern era.

Irony stems from a realization that no narrative or practice has universal and absolute validity (McGuiness 1997: 29–44; Rorty 1989; Seglow 1996: 41–43). But such a realization can generate a different mood of excitement and carnival; a feeling that at last anything is possible and that we have the right and capacity to make the world as we desire. We know, at last, that as in stories, we can also change our readings of roles and narrate for ourselves. We know there is no safe port nor a final destination, but this frees us to argue over what we wish for and set sail where we wish. We are not the displaced nomads and travellers typified by Bauman, but more or less intrepid explorers and makers of maps. We are less engaged in disengagement and displacement activity and more likely to be engaged in identity formation and expressive activity. Like the Renaissance, postmodernity offers not only a critique of the past but a new set of narratives for the future, many of which can be entertained without angst and indeed can be celebrated. Like Renaissance humanists, postmodernists are happier doing it now than aiming for it in the future, happier expressing than realizing, happier acting than contemplating, happier performing than being entertained.

Achievement in postmodern politics will remain ever contingent and transient. Dangers will remain of uncontrolled multi-national capital, ecological risk and tribal political violence. Worklessness and global injustice will not be eradicated, but should not distract from an optimistic conclusion. Never before have so many people in the world had the knowledge, power and intention to make capital and political power serve their own aims. Kaase and Newton summarize what we know about what has happened to citizens and politics since the Second World War: 'Citizens have become more educated, more politically involved, and more active' at the same time as becoming 'more individualistic, more self centred, more wedded to the specific interests of their immediate group', and parties and government are having to adapt (1995:170). While things other than politics will continue to attract the attention and time of postmodernists, it is the case that they will engage in politics more confidently whenever it facilitates the other desires and achievements they entertain. We may conclude, then, that while the process of postmodernization will bring mixed blessings, it does allow unrivalled opportunities for the lives of individuals and groups to change. Secondly, that while change offers plural and contested futures, if citizens can be encouraged to take advantage of the new resources and opportunities made available to reinvent their worlds, postmodern change will be more reflexive, more in the control of agents, and more open to public control via democratic politics. That is the progressive potential of postmodernity.

Postscript:
The Future of Political Science

How can political science respond to the challenges posed by postmodernity? This question divides into two others: (1) How do we do political science in postmodernity? And (2) How do we organize the political science profession in postmodernity? Answers to these questions will depend upon how we define the key concepts 'political', 'postmodern', 'political science' and 'professional'. The first two have been analysed extensively above, but we must comment on the latter two. By political science can be meant the narrow field of empirical and positivistic studies of politics that have blossomed since the 1950s in American and Western European political science and government departments, associated with such figures as Almond, Blondel, Dahl, Easton, Lasswell, Lipset, Parsons, Rokkan and Verba – all men. At the other end of the spectrum political science is the general term for the whole family of disciplines and approaches that study politics, in political theory, philosophy, sociology, psychology, history, management, geography, social policy, criminology, media and cultural studies – many led by women.

We intend to answer the question in regard to the second definition. By a profession we mean an occupational grouping established by its varying ability to monopolize a specialist skill and service provision; by the recognition that it can control entry, training, discipline and exit; and that it is allowed to regulate itself by having its own code of conduct, impose its own standards, and transmit a common culture to its members.

Postmodern discourse, we argued, arises both from changes in the way we look at the world and from changes in the world. We may summarize the new challenge for a postmodern political science by two arguments: the epistemological world of modern political science has changed, and so has that modern world it studies (Gibbins and Reimer 1995). In summary, many political scientists are somewhere along the line of abandoning empiricism, foundationalism, universalism and the idea of academic neutrality in epistemology, and they find themselves studying a world where the older practices, institutions and belief systems associated with modern liberal democracies seem to be undergoing radical and asystemic change.

Epistemologically, postmodernists are moving to explore how we can study this new world by embracing contemporary trends towards neo-idealist hermeneutic epistemologies, towards an array of anti-foundational hermeneutic or phenomenological methods, and by a commitment to study the diverse and the particular – alongside a realization that knowledge is connected to power in newer and deeper ways. We must also consider reinventions of old actors in politics, as well as acknowledging new actors, values, allegiances, behaviours, structures, parties, movements, processes and organizations – locally, nationally and globally.

A number of new directions for political science seem to be emerging from this encounter with postmodernism, all of which suggest that a restructuring or reinvention metaphor may be appropriate to characterize the situation. Although most of our examples arc British, we consider that the restructurings to which we refer have applications to the wider Western world. At the heart is the abandonment of the idea that political science is a unitary study with a consensus on methods. Most departments today are recognizably multi-disciplinary and multi-paradigmatic and will continue to be so for the foreseeable future. Next, political science is today abandoning the enterprise of defending discipline boundaries and is entering the less chartered waters of inter- and multi-disciplinary study. It is now the norm for scholars to have to understand the languages of many, if not all, of the disciplines listed above, so political historians today, much to the chagrin of Oakeshott, must respond to the language and agenda of sociologists who study movements, professionalization and postmodernization; to media and cultural theorists studying construction and representation; to gender theorists studying feminism and masculinities; and to poststructuralist philosophers such as Foucault and Lyotard.

Whereas critical analysis is the basis of all modern political science, the art of deconstruction is newer and more profound. Here the minimal aim is to challenge and deny the binaries around which political science is constructed – binaries such as science/arts, public/private, political/moral, legal/criminal, legitimate/subversive – as have feminists and critical theorists, and then to explore various points inbetween. Concerted deconstruction would seek to challenge the whole vocabulary of political science in order to reveal implicit values, the power implied by knowledge, and the exclusionary effects of various discourses. As postmodernism is shaped so centrally by the new philosophies of language, we envisage that political science will be shaped in the future by the explicit rather than implicit application of linguistic devices, and by the study of discourses, voices, vocabularies, texts, authors, canons, genres, conversations and dialogical methods.

The acceptance of the relationship of knowledge/ power in political science should lead to a rewriting of the history of the subject, and especially the unearthing of the economic, political and social contexts accompanying the development of its agenda, and of the manipulative role of intellectuals and other professionals. Just as feminists have unearthed the male nature of political science, and post-colonialists are unearthing the imperialistic character of Western political science, so will we need to go on and rewrite our history from the vantage point of other excluded minority groups. The changing of the political science canon should follow on from this endeavour so that minor pamphleteers, journalists, union officials and activists will gain the same status in the canon as members of representative assemblies and academics. We will need to look at the abuses as well as the uses of political science and its poor track record of assisting the already powerful and handicapping the excluded.

This will direct us to new sites for study, beyond those contained in the core subjects in most political science undergraduate programmes. We should expect the whole gamut of excluded groups, processes of exclusion and writing out of history to be made visible, such as modules on gay politics; animal rights; film, novels, art, music and the media; the study of the politics involved in school curriculum, newspapers and magazines; doctors' surgeries, shopping malls, supermarkets, public toilets; motor vehicles, the countryside, food production and reprocessing, tourism, sexuality, clothing and our bodies (Gibbins 1998b). It is likely that a vast amount of research will go into understanding the consumers of politics; the readers of the political texts presented by key actors.

We expect the study of political values and cultures will develop to provide insight into the way that both actors and consumers of politics are constructed and construct in turn. Political culture and the study of values, preferences and ethics should extrude formerly central concerns like political behaviour, class, ideology and power. Similarly, we expect the study of political aesthetics and style to become central in a world where simulation and the simulated are so intricately intertwined.

On methods we should expect the present explosion of types and styles so effectively found in feminism and cultural studies to continue. Methods formerly considered mutually exclusive, such as the empirical and theoretical, the comparative and the psychological, the qualitative and the quantitative, will be bound together in eclectic mixes that will survive if they work in hermeneutic terms. We should expect that just as the language and methods of literary studies and discourse analysis have now penetrated political science successfully, we may expect the same from other disciplines and fields of study, each taking turns to nourish or strangle the other.

Sceptical postmodernists will contend that as there is no correct method for political research and researching the political, we must adopt an 'anti-rules' method, while the affirmatives may adopt an 'anything goes' approach. Feyerabend's book title *Against Method:*

Outlines of an Anarchistic Theory of Knowledge (1975), seems to be the best example of the former approach, while Giddens' *New Rules of Sociological Method* (1976) and the eclectic collection *Theory and Methods in Political Science* (1995), edited by Marsh and Stoker, illustrate the second. For ourselves we promote an approach best described as 'horses for courses', the idea that several methodologies may well need to be blended together to provide the best method to researching a problem. We should embrace this – along with openness and reflexivity – and reject all demands that research and researchers conform to any one research strategy. This amounts to more than 'anything goes' (Heller 1986; Rorty 1979: 318; Rosenau 1992: 116–127). We argue that 'more goes' better captures the postmodern attitude to methodology.

A key conceptual link between postmodern method and theory is the tendency towards subjectivity, particularity and relativism, and away from objectivism, universalism and absolutism in their most extreme forms. Postmodernists are inclined to start with the particular forms of life and life-worlds of particular individuals and groups, and to favour methods of introspection, ethnography and interpretation. That an infinite number of life-worlds and interpretations are possible prevents ascription to any idea of final or ultimate knowledge as advanced in the Enlightenment, and by positivists and Fukuyama (1992) since. The lessons of literary studies dominate much of modern social sciences at present – notions of authors, readers, readings, texts, genres, narratives and canons – and we expect the import of methods from other fields to continue. That this may amount to a method itself is hard to contest, but it is a different, more open, critical and reflexive method. What it rejects is the grounding of a research project in one methodology or paradigm, such as positivism, Marxism or feminism. Postmodern feminists were the first postmodernists to reject the essentialist foundations of other variants of feminism and have shown the way forward (Fraser 1989; Fraser and Nicholson 1988; Nicholson 1990; Shildrich 1997). As well as deconstructing theories, multi-theories will be constructed. That it will not be a purely destructive method should become apparent (Habermas 1987: 161).

Political theory is already fully immersed in the experience of pluralization, differentiation and eclecticism found in cultural studies. Conference agendas and programmes will continue these trends and will see the incorporation of new theories from other disciplines and fields of study. However, theory will be entwined in a different way with practice, prescription and prognosis than was acceptable in modern political science. Whereas the founding Directors of the London School of Economics, such as Tawney, Laski and Beveridge, were promoting modernist and Fordist political projects such as the welfare state, the present incumbent, Anthony Giddens, plays a very different role, entrepreneurial, mercurial, journalistic – in short postmodern (Giddens 1998). A postmodern political scientist will not play at neutrality, but his or her loyalties and engagements will not be predictable and stable over time. Postmodernists will prescribe, but not necessarily for the good of central interests. Above all, political scientists must respond to the question of why they buy into the theories, explanations, understandings and languages they do, and need to look for non-structuralist and non-determinist answers that may allow for more engaged practices.

This brings us finally to question (2) around organization of the profession of political science, its research centres, departments, schools, professional bodies, journals, training, codes of conduct and culture. University academics had a monopoly on the political science profession until the late nineteenth century in Britain, but since then, under the impact of state policy to expand higher education, this has slowly been eroded. A process of de-professionalization was engendered as the state imposed control on the universities via funding bodies; conditions of entry, curriculum and training, fees and salaries, quality assessment of teaching and research, control on budgets and the research agendas via the activities of Research Councils. At the same time, university academics have fought to re-professionalize, using all the techniques listed by Foucault in aid of this project of knowledge/power: monopolization; creation of an episteme, mentality and discourse; surveillance, discipline and control (MacDonald 1995: 174–186). The rise of the big national professional associations of political scientists, with their annual conventions, bureaucracies, journals and lines of communication, their professional codes and political advocacy, illustrates this process. While the conflict between these processes of de- and re-professionalization is not and perhaps will not be resolved, we may provide an interpretation from a postmodern perspective.

Modernization, as Weber informs us, was premised upon rationalization of life, including the professions. The aspects of professions that modern states hated the most have been the pervasive and residual traditionalism at their centres. The professionalization of law, teaching, banking, the civil service, the police, army, clergy and architecture in the nineteenth century was conducted in a way that allowed culture and friendship to dominate. Commercialism, utilitarianism and instrumentalism took second place to these factors. The contemporary attack on professions by New Right politicians, under the guise of an attack upon commercial monopoly, can be interpreted as a late modern attempt to rationalize the professions and impose a competitive entrepreneurial commercial ethos upon them. Alternatively, it can be interpreted as a necessary deconstructive attack on the knowledge/power processes that postmodernists encourage. The critical work by feminists such as Witz (1992) on exposing the patriarchal tenets of professions may act as a precursor of what may come in future work on the professions. We expect that the role, status and power of excluded groups, the part-time lecturers, post-graduate students, contract researchers will be renegotiated to provide greater inclusion (Doyle and McGregor-Riley 1996).

For us the fact that professions did not conform to Weber's notion of rationalization is evidence that no unilinear or universalistic account of professions will stand up to rigorous study. The current attack by The New Right on professions illustrates one effect of postmodernization: the demand that all services become able to operate in a flexible global commercial and consumer market. The work of feminists illustrates some future directions for postmodern research on professions focusing on the exclusory regimes and impacts of the operation on professional bodies (Witz 1992).

What our work on expressivism suggests is that we need to make political science a more open, reflexive and dialogical profession. Pyramidal organizations are giving way either to flatter alternatives or, as Rhodes

(1996) suggests, to interlinked and self-managed networks that need less central governance. Political scientists in postmodernity will not take easily to old-style Fordist management and will prefer some more post-Fordist alternatives (Burrows and Loader 1994; Rhodes 1996). Within academic departments it is becoming obvious that common collegiate culture and practice is harder to evoke. Most departments are loose confederations of individuals more or less internally and externally networked. Networking and being networked are now perhaps the most important determinants of the success of both academics and their departments – if we overlook the presentation, representation and reproduction of signs of prestige and achievement. University departments may wish to recognize and facilitate this in their own management of affairs. The provision of resources, resource allocation, policy making and implementation should reflect the global/local nature of political science and allow a variety of sub-organizations to bloom with self-managed budgets, all co-ordinated via regular reviews of missions and achievements and conformity to ethical standards, rather than direct and permanent regulation.

Allowing self-management should be accompanied by a recognition of differences and distinctions in organizations. That there is no right way to run a department or research centre should allow and encourage a variety of types and styles of management rather than impose a corporate model. Plurality, not monopoly, and a concern to establish and practise a code of ethics should inform the corporate strategy. Networking will be facilitated by the use of all available types of information transfer, and political organizations must ensure they are well placed to reflect the kind of information- or cyber-democracy that is planned for the public world. Being networked by user groups, mailing lists, web sites and subject mail groups are just some of the tools departments must ensure political scientists can access, utilize and set up for others.

Such a strategy would allow the bringing of new groups and formerly excluded groups of users into departments and debates. The opening of departments and centres to the community in its widest sense is a strategy to encourage, and will need a particular type of organization to accommodate. The modernist dichotomies of professional/practitioner, professional/client and profession/public will have to be permeated to facilitate the revised and wider role of political science conjectured above. Political activists and practitioners should be able to use political scientists as a resource. Departments will need to be networked with the movements and bodies they formerly stood outside to explain. Already this is happening around areas concerned with energy, the environment and feminism, but needs to be extended to voluntary associations, new age groups and movements around sexualities (Heelas 1996).

Within professional bodies, several lines of organizational change are indicated by a postmodern approach. National bodies should become more like new states, devolving power and budgets to small sub-groups and networks and sharing national remits and agendas with other national and international bodies, such as the Association of Learned Societies in the Social Sciences (ALSSS) and the Academy for Social Sciences (ASS) in Britain. Centrifugal pressures are resulting in the mushrooming of smaller specialist professional organizations, journals and networks, such as the Political Theory Collective at Oxford with its links to the Conference for the Study of Political Thought centred now at the University of Colorado, with the attendant danger that generalist national bodies will lose legitimacy. In Britain the Political Science Association recognizes this trend and has responded by expanding the list of specialist study groups, and by its co-operation with a transnational body like the European Consortium for Political Research, other national bodies such as the American Political Science Association, and international bodies such as the International Political Science Association.

Sharing, co-operating and joint funding rather than protecting, competing and budgetary sovereignty seem better ways towards realizing a postmodern political science profession. Political science needs to be a world-wide profession, and it has to make its discursive practices more widely available. Making it world-wide while encouraging access and responsiveness to the agenda of expressive individuals and groups, to practitioner groupings and the formerly excluded, all within a customer service policy that is highly inclusive, is the agenda for the future postmodern profession of political science.

References

Anderson, Benedict (1991) *Imagined Communities: Reflections on the Origin and Spread of Nationalism*. (Revised edition.) London: Verso.

Andersson, Magnus and André Jansson (1997) 'Media Use and Cultural Identity: Results and Reflections from an Interview Study in Two Different Parts of Gothenburg'. Paper Presented at the 13th Nordic Conference on Mass Communication Research, Jyväskylä, Finland.

Ang, Ien (1985) *Watching Dallas: Soap Opera and the Melodramatic Imagination*. London: Methuen.

Anglo, Sidney (1969) *Machiavelli: A Dissection*. London: Gollancz.

Appadurai, Arjun (1990) 'Disjuncture and Difference in the Global Cultural Economy', in M. Featherstone (ed.), *Global Culture: Nationalism, Globalization and Modernity*. London: Sage.

Avineri, Shlomo and Avner de-Shalit (1992) *Communitarianism and Liberalism*. Oxford: Oxford University Press.

Barnes, Samuel and Max Kaase (1979) *Political Action: Mass Participation in Five Western Democracies*. London: Sage.

Baudrillard, Jean (1981) *For a Critique of the Political Economy of the Sign*. St Louis, MO: Telos Press.

Baudrillard, Jean (1983) *Simulations*. New York: Semiotext(e).

Baudrillard, Jean (1984) 'On Nihilism', *On the Beach*, 6: 38–39.

Baudrillard, Jean (1988) *America*. London: Verso.

Bauman, Zygmunt (1991) *Modernity and Ambivalence*. Cambridge: Polity Press.

Bauman, Zygmunt (1992) *Intimations of Postmodernity*. London: Routledge.

Bauman, Zygmunt (1993) *Postmodern Ethics*. Oxford: Blackwell.

Bauman, Zygmunt (1997) *Postmodernity and its Discontents*. Cambridge: Polity Press.

Bausinger, Herman (1984) 'Media, Technology and Daily Life', *Media, Culture and Society*, 6: 343–351.

Beck, Ulrich (1992) *Risk Society: Towards a New Modernity*. London: Sage.

Beck, Ulrich (1996) *The Reinvention of Politics*. Cambridge: Polity Press.

Beck, Ulrich (1997) *Democracy*. Cambridge: Polity Press.

Beck, Ulrich, Anthony Giddens and Scott Lash (1994) *Reflexive*

Modernization: Politics, Tradition and Aesthetics in the Modern Social Order. Cambridge: Polity Press.

Beiner, Ronald (1995) *Theorizing Citizenship*. Albany: State University of New York Press.

Bell, Daniel (1960) *The End of Ideology*. New York: Free Press.

Bell, Daniel (1973) *The Coming of Post-Industrial Society*. New York: Basic Books.

Bellah, Robert N., Richard Madsen, William M. Sullivan, Ann Swidler and Steven M. Tipton (1985) *Habits of the Heart: Individualism and Commitment in American Life*. Berkeley: University of California Press.

Bellamy, Richard (1992) *Liberalism and Modern Society*. Cambridge: Polity Press.

Benhabib, Seyla (1992) *Situating the Self: Gender, Community and Postmodernism in Contemporary Ethics*. Cambridge: Polity Press.

Berger, Peter, Brigitte Berger and Hansfried Kellner (1974) *The Homeless Mind: Modernization and Consciousness*. New York: Vintage Books.

Berlin, Isaiah (1969) *Four Essays on Liberty*. Oxford: Oxford University Press.

Berman, Marshall (1982) *All That is Solid Melts into Air: The Experience of Modernity*. New York: Simon and Schuster.

Bertens, Hans (1995) *The Idea of the Postmodern*. London: Routledge.

Best, Steven and Douglas Kellner (1991) *Postmodern Theory: Critical Interrogations*. London: Macmillan.

Blaug, Ricardo (1996) 'New Developments in Deliberative Democracy', *Politics*, 16: 71–77.

Blumler, Jay G. and Michael Gurevitch (1995) *The Crisis of Public Communication*. London: Routledge.

Blumler, Jay G. and Elihu Katz (eds) (1974) *The Uses of Mass Communications: Current Perspectives*. Beverly Hills: Sage.

Bobbio, Norberto (1987) *The Future of Democracy*. Cambridge: Polity Press.

Bobbio, Norberto (1996) *Left and Right: The Significance of a Political Distinction*. Cambridge: Polity Press.

Bobbio, Norberto (1997) *Democracy and Dictatorship: The Nature and Limits of State Power*. Cambridge: Polity Press.

Bocock, Robert (1992) 'Consumption and Lifestyles', in R. Bocock and K. Thompson (eds), *Social and Cultural Forms of Modernity*. Cambridge: Polity Press.

Boëthius, Ulf (1995) 'The History of High and Low Culture', in J. Fornäs and G. Bolin (eds), *Youth Culture in Late Modernity*. London: Sage.

References

Borre, Ole and Elinor Scarbrough (eds.) (1995) *The Scope of Government*. Oxford: Oxford University Press.

Botwinick, Aryeh (1993) *Postmodernism and Democratic Theory*. Philadelphia: Temple University Press.

Bourdieu, Pierre (1984) *Distinction: A Social Critique of the Judgement of Taste*. Cambridge, MA: Harvard University Press.

Boyne, Roy (1995) *Foucault and Derrida*. London: Macmillan.

Brittan, Samuel (1977) *The Economic Consequences of Democracy*. London: Temple Smith.

Brown, Seyon (1988) *New Forces, Old Forces and the Future of World Politics*. Glenview, IL: Scott, Foresman and Company.

Bryant, Jennings and Dolf Zillman (eds.) (1994) *Media Effects: Advances in Theory and Research*. Hillsdale, NJ: Lawrence Erlbaum.

Budge, Ian (1996) *The New Challenge of Direct Democracy*. Cambridge: Polity Press.

Bull, Hedley (1977) *The Anarchical Society*. London: Macmillan.

Bull, Hedley and Adam Watson (eds.) (1984) *The Expansion of International Society*. Oxford: Clarendon.

Burnett, Robert (1996) *The Global Jukebox: The International Music Industry in Transition*. London: Routledge.

Burrows, Roger and Brian Loader (eds.) (1994) *Towards a Post-Fordist Welfare State*. London: Routledge.

Butler, Judith (1997) *Excitable Speech: The Politics of the Performative*. London: Routledge.

Cahoone, Lawrence (ed.) (1996) *From Modern to Post-Modern: Postmodernism in Context*. Oxford: Blackwell.

Carey, James (1989) *Communication as Culture: Essays on Media and Society*. London: Unwin Hyman.

Carter, John (ed.) (1998) *Postmodernity and the Fragmentation of Welfare*. London: Routledge.

Callan, Eamon (1997) *Creating Citizenship*. Oxford: Oxford University Press.

Cawson, Alan (1986) *Corporatism and Political Theory*. Oxford: Blackwell.

Cerny, Philip G. (1990) *The Changing Architecture of Politics: Structure, Agency and the Future of the State*. London: Sage.

de Certeau, Michel (1984) *The Practice of Everyday Life*. Berkeley: University of California Press.

Chaney, David (1996) *Lifestyles*. London: Routledge.

Cochrane, Alan (1998) 'Globalization, Fragmentation and Local Welfare', in J. Carter (ed.), *Postmodernity and the Fragmentation of Welfare*. London: Routledge.

Connolly, William (1983) *The Terms of Political Discourse*. 2nd edition. Oxford: Martin Robertson.

Connolly, William (1988) *Political Theory and Modernity*. Oxford: Blackwell.

Connolly, William (1991) *Identity/Difference: Democratic Negotiations of Political Paradox*. Ithaca, NY: Cornell University Press.

Connolly, William (1995) *The Ethics of Pluralization*. Minneapolis: University of Minneapolis Press.

Cooper, Robert (1996) *The Post-Modern State and the World Order*. London: Demos.

Crook, Stephen, Jan Pakulski and Malcolm Waters (1992) *Postmodernization: Change in Advanced Society*. London: Sage.

Crouch, Colin and David Marquand (eds.) (1995) *Reinventing Collective Action*. Oxford: Blackwell.

Dagger, Richard (1997) *Civic Virtues: Rights, Citizenship and Republican Liberalism*. Oxford: Oxford University Press.

Dalton, Russell (1988) *Citizen Politics in Western Democracies*. Chatham, NJ: Chatham House.

Dayan, Daniel and Elihu Katz (1992) *Media Events: The Live Broadcasting of History*. Cambridge, MA: Harvard University Press.

Dearing, James W. and Everett M. Rogers (1996) *Agenda-Setting*. Thousand Oaks, CA: Sage.

d'Entreve, Maurizio (1994) *The Political Philosophy of Hannah Arendt*. London: Routledge.

Derrida, Jacques (1982) *Margins of Philosophy*. Brighton: Harvester.

Digeser, Peter (1995) *Our Politics, Our Selves? Liberalism, Identity, and Harm*. Princeton: Princeton University Press.

Doyle, Helen and Victoria McGregor-Riley (1996) 'Political Science: A Look at the Discipline from a Postgraduate Perspective', *Politics*, 16: 113–120.

Dunn, John (ed.) (1994) 'Contemporary Crisis of the Nation State, Special Issue', *Political Studies*, 42: 3–15.

Edelman, Murray (1988) *Constructing the Political Spectacle*. Chicago: University of Chicago Press.

Eisenstadt, S.N. (1987) 'Introduction: Historical Traditions, Modernization and Development', in S.N. Eisenstadt (ed.), *Patterns of Modernity: Volume 1. The West*. London: Frances Pinter.

Everard, Jerry (1998) *Virtual States: Globalization, Inequality and the Internet*. London: Routledge.

Featherstone, Mike (1985) 'The Fate of Modernity: An Introduction', *Theory, Culture & Society*, 2(3): 1–5.

182

References

Featherstone, Mike (1988) 'In Pursuit of the Postmodern', *Theory, Culture & Society*, 5(2–3): 195–215.

Featherstone, Mike (1991) *Consumer Culture and Postmodernism*. London: Sage.

Featherstone, Mike, Scott Lash and Roland Robertson (eds.) (1995) *Global Modernities*. London: Sage.

Feyerabend, Paul K. (1975) *Against Method*. London: New Left Books.

Fiske, John (1987) *Television Culture*. London: Methuen.

Fiske, John (1989) *Understanding Popular Culture*. Boston: Unwin Hyman.

Fiske, John (1996) *Media Matters: Race and Gender in US Politics*. Revised edition. Minneapolis: University of Minnesota Press.

Flax, Jane (1987) 'Postmodernism and Gender Relations in Feminist Theory', *Signs*, 12: 621–643.

Flax, Jane (1993) *Disputed Subjects: Essays on Psychoanalysis, Politics and Philosophy*. London: Routledge.

Foot, Philippa (1967) 'Moral Beliefs', in P. Foot (ed.), *Theories of Ethics*, Oxford: Oxford University Press.

Fornäs, Johan (1995) *Cultural Theory and Late Modernity*. London: Sage.

Foster, Hal (1995) 'Expressionism', in F. Frascini and J. Harris (eds.), *Art in Modern Culture*. London: Phaidon.

Fox, C.J. and H.T. Miller (1995) *Postmodern Public Administration: Towards Discourse*. London: Sage.

Fraser, Nancy (1989) *Unruly Practices: Power, Discourse and Gender in Contemporary Social Theory*. Cambridge: Polity Press.

Fraser, Nancy and Linda Nicholson (1988) 'Social Criticism without Philosophy: An Encounter between Feminism and Postmodernism', *Theory, Culture & Society*, 5: 374–394.

Fukuyama, Francis (1992) *The End of History and the Last Man*. Harmondsworth: Penguin.

Gallie, W.B. (1955–1956/1962) 'Essentially Contested Concepts', in M. Black (ed.), *The Importance of Language*. Englewood, NJ: Prentice Hall.

Gamman, Lorraine and Merja Makinen (1994) *Female Fetishism: A New Look*. London: Lawrence and Wishart.

García Canclini, Néstor (1995) *Hybrid Cultures: Strategies for Entering and Leaving Modernity*. Minneapolis: University of Minnesota Press.

Gibbins, John (1989a) 'Contemporary Political Culture: An Introduction', in J. Gibbins (ed.), *Contemporary Political Culture: Politics in a Postmodern Age*. London: Sage.

Gibbins, John (ed.) (1989b) *Contemporary Political Culture: Politics in a Postmodern Age*. London: Sage.

Gibbins, John (1990) 'The New State and the Impact of Values'. Unpublished paper, European Science Foundation.

Gibbins, John (1998a) 'Postmodernism, Poststructuralism and Social Policy', in J. Carter (ed.), *Postmodernity and the Fragmentation of Welfare*. London: Routledge.

Gibbins, John (1998b) 'Sexuality and the Law: The Body in Politics', in T. Carver and V. Mottier (eds), *Politics of Sexuality*. London: Routledge.

Gibbins, John and Bo Reimer (1995) 'Postmodernism', in J. van Deth and E. Scarbrough (eds), *The Impact of Values*. Oxford: Oxford University Press.

Gibbins, John and Bo Reimer (1998) 'Lifestyles', *Working Paper*. Gothenburg: Department of Journalism and Mass Communication, Gothenburg University.

Gibson, Carol and Roma Gibson (1993) *Dirty Looks: Women, Pornography, Power*. London: British Film Institute.

Giddens, Anthony (1976) *New Rules of Sociological Method*. London: Hutchinson.

Giddens, Anthony (1984) *The Constitution of Society*. Cambridge: Polity Press.

Giddens, Anthony (1990) *The Consequences of Modernity*. Cambridge: Polity Press.

Giddens, Anthony (1991) *Modernity and Self-Identity: Self and Society in the Late Modern Age*. Cambridge: Polity Press.

Giddens, Anthony (1992) *The Transformation of Intimacy*. Cambridge: Polity Press.

Giddens, Anthony (1994) *Beyond Left and Right: The Future of Radical Politics*. Cambridge: Polity Press.

Giddens, Anthony (1997) *Critical Assessments*. London: Heinemann.

Giddens, Anthony (1998) *The Third Way: The Renewal of Social Democracy*. Cambridge: Polity Press.

Gladwin, Maree (1994) 'The Theory and Politics of Contemporary Social Movements', *Politics*, 14: 59–65.

Gray, John (1996) *Enlightenment's Wake: Politics and Culture at the End of the Modern Age*. London: Routledge.

Gray, John (1997) *Endgames: Questions in Late Modern Political Thought*. Cambridge: Polity Press.

Grosz, Elizabeth and Elspeth Probyn (1995) *Sexy Bodies: The Strange Carnalities of Feminism*. London: Routledge.

Grote, John (1870) *An Examination of the Utilitarian Philosophy*. Cambridge: Deighton and Bell.

Grote, John (1876) *A Treatise on the Moral Ideals*. Cambridge: Cambridge University Press.

References

Gundelach, Peter (1992) 'Recent Value Changes in Western Europe', *Futures*, May, 301–319.

Haber, Honi F. (1994) *Beyond Postmodern Politics: Lyotard, Rorty, Foucault*. London: Routledge.

Habermas, Jürgen (1962/1989) *The Structural Transformation of the Public Sphere: An Inquiry into a Category of Bourgeois Society*. Cambridge: Polity Press.

Habermas, Jürgen (1976) *Legitimation Crisis*. London: Heinemann.

Habermas, Jürgen (1987) *The Theory of Communicative Action, Volume 2*. Boston: Beacon Press.

Habermas, Jürgen (1990) *The Philosophical Discourse of Modernity*. Cambridge: Polity Press.

Hall, John (1989) *The State*. Oxford: Oxford University Press.

Hall, John (ed.) (1995) *Civil Society: Theory, History, Comparison*. Oxford: Polity Press.

Hall, Stuart (1992) 'The Question of Cultural Identity', in S. Hall, D. Held and T. McGrew (eds) *Modernity and its Futures*. Cambridge: Polity Press.

Hall, Stuart and Bram Gieben (eds) (1992) *Formations of Modernity*. Cambridge: Polity Press.

Hamelink, Cees (1983) *Cultural Autonomy in Global Communications*. New York: Longman.

Harvey, David (1989) *The Condition of Postmodernity: An Enquiry into the Origins of Cultural Change*. Oxford: Basil Blackwell.

Hassan, Ihab (1971/1982) *The Dismemberment of Orpheus: Towards a Postmodern Literature*. 2nd edition. London: University of Wisconsin Press.

Hassan, Ihab (1985) 'The Culture of Postmodernism', *Theory, Culture & Society*, 2: 119–131.

Heckman, Susan J. (1990) *Elements of a Postmodern Feminism*. Boston: Northeastern University Press.

Heelas, Paul (1996) *New Age Movements*. Oxford: Blackwell.

Heelas, Paul, Scott Lash and Paul Morris (1995) *Detraditionalization*. Oxford: Blackwell.

Held, David (1989) *Political Theory and the Modern State*. Cambridge: Polity Press.

Held, David (ed.) (1993) *Prospects for Democracy: North, South, East, West*. Cambridge: Polity Press.

Held, David (1995a) 'Democracy and the New World Order', in D. Held and D. Archibugi (eds), *Cosmopolitan Democracy: An Agenda for a New World Order*. Cambridge: Polity Press.

Held, David (1995b) *Democracy and the Global Order: From Modern State to Cosmopolitan Governance*. Cambridge: Polity Press.

Held, David and Danielle Archibugi (eds) (1995) *Cosmopolitan Democracy: An Agenda for a New World Order*. Cambridge: Polity Press.

Heller, Agnes and Ferenc Feher (1989) *The Postmodern Political Condition*. Oxford: Blackwell.

Heller, Ferenc (ed.) (1986) *The Use and Abuse of Social Science*. London: Sage.

Hirst, Paul (1994) *Associative Democracy*. Cambridge: Polity Press.

Hirst, Paul and Sunil Khilnani (eds) (1996) *Reinventing Democracy*. Oxford: Blackwell.

Hoffman, John (1995) *Beyond the State*. Oxford: Polity Press.

Hudnut, Joseph (1945) 'The Postmodern House', *Architectural Record*, 97: 70–75.

Inglehart, Ronald (1977) *The Silent Revolution: Changing Values and Political Styles among Western Democracies*. Princeton: Princeton University Press.

Inglehart, Ronald (1990) *Culture Shift in Advanced Industrial Societies*. Princeton: Princeton University Press.

Inglehart, Ronald and Peter Abramson (1994) 'Economic Security and Value Change', *American Political Science Review*, 88: 336–354.

Jagodzinski, Wolfgang and Karel Dobbelaere (1995) 'Religious and Ethical Pluralism', in J. van Deth and E. Scarbrough (eds), *The Impact of Values*. Oxford: Oxford University Press.

Jahn, Detlef (1989) 'Changes in the Political Culture – Challenges to the Trade Union Movement: The Debate on Nuclear Energy in Swedish and German Trade Unions', in J. Gibbins (ed.), *Contemporary Political Culture: Politics in a Postmodern Age*. London: Sage.

Jameson, Fredric (1989) 'Marxism and Postmodernism', *New Left Review*, 176: 31–45.

Jameson, Fredric (1991) *Postmodernism, or the Cultural Logic of Late Capitalism*. London: Verso.

Jansson, André (1998) *Contested Meanings: Audience Studies and the Concept of Cultural Identity*. Paper Presented at the 2nd Crossroads in Cultural Studies Conference, Tampere, Finland.

Jennings, M. Kent and Jan van Deth et al. (1989) *Continuities in Political Action*. Berlin: de Gruyter.

Jessop, Bob (1982) *The Capitalist State*. Oxford: Martin Robertson.

Johnson, Leslie (1981) 'Radio and Everyday Life: The Early Years of Broadcasting', *Media, Culture and Society*, 3: 167–178.

Kaase, Max and Ken Newton (1995) *Beliefs in Government*. Oxford: Oxford University Press.

186

References

King, Anthony D. (ed.) (1991) *Culture, Globalization and the World-System*. Binghamton: Dept of Art and Art History, State University of New York at Binghamton.

King, Anthony D. (1995) 'The Times and Spaces of Modernity (or Who Needs Postmodernism?)', in M. Featherstone, S. Lash and R. Robertson (eds), *Global Modernities*. London: Sage.

Klages, Helmut and Willie Herbert (1983) *Wertorientierung und Staatsbezug: Untersuchungen zur Politischen Kultur in der Bundesrepublik Deutschland*. Frankfurt: Campus.

Kleinig, John (1996) *The Ethics of Policing*. Cambridge: Cambridge University Press.

Klingemann, Hans-Dieter and Dieter Fuchs (eds) (1995) *Citizens and the State*. Oxford: Oxford University Press.

Kratz, Charlotta and Bo Reimer (1998) 'Fashion in the Face of Postmodernity', in A.A. Berger (ed.), *The Postmodern Presence: Readings on Postmodernism in American Culture and Society*. Walnut Creek, CA: AltaMira Press.

Kroker, Arthur and David Cook (1988) *The Postmodern Scene: Excremental Culture and Hyper-Aesthetics*. London: Macmillan.

Kumar, Krishan (1978) *Prophecy and Progress: The Sociology of Industrial and Post-Industrial Society*. Harmondsworth: Pelican.

Kumar, Krishan (1995) *From Post-Industrial to Post-Modern Society: New Theories of the Contemporary World*. Oxford: Blackwell.

Kymlicka, William (1990) *Contemporary Political Philosophy*. Oxford: Oxford University Press.

Kymlicka, William (1995) *Multicultural Citizenship*. Oxford: Clarendon.

Kymlicka, William (1997) 'Do We Need a Liberal Theory of Minority Rights? Reply to Carens, Young, Parekh and Forst', *New Constellation*, 4: 72–87.

Lacey, Nancy and Elizabeth Frazer (1994) 'Communitarianism', *Politics*, 14: 75–81.

Laclau, Ernesto (1990) *New Reflections on the Revolution of our Times*. London: Verso.

Laclau, Ernesto and Mouffe, Chantal (1985) *Hegemony and Socialist Strategy*. London: Verso.

Laermans, R. (1992) *In der greet van 'De moderne tijd'*, *Modernisering En verzuiling: Evoluies binner de ACU – Vormingsorganisaties*. Leuven: Appeldoorn Garant.

Lash, Scott and John Urry (1987) *The End of Organized Capitalism*. Cambridge: Polity Press.

Lash, Scott and John Urry (1994) *Economies of Signs and Space*. London: Sage.

Lemert, Charles (1992) 'General Social Theory, Irony, Postmodernism', in S. Seidman and D.G. Wagner (eds), *Postmodernism and Social Theory*. Oxford: Blackwell.

Leonard, Peter (1997) *Postmodern Welfare: Reconstructing an Emancipatory Project*. London: Sage.

Liebes, Tamar and Elihu Katz (1990) *The Export of Meaning: Cross-Cultural Readings of Dallas*. New York: Oxford University Press.

Livingstone, Sonia (1996) 'On the Continuing Problem of Media Effects', in J. Curran and M. Gurevitch (eds), *Mass Media and Society*. 2nd edition. London: Arnold.

Loader, Brian (ed.) (1997) *The Governance of Cyberspace: Politics, Technology and Global Restructuring*. London: Routledge.

Loader, Brian (ed.) (1998) *Cyberspace Divide: Agency, Equality and Autonomy in the Information Society*. London: Routledge.

Lull, James (1990) *Inside Family Viewing: Ethnographic Research on Television's Audiences*. London: Routledge.

Lull, James (1995) *Media, Communication, Culture: A Global Approach*. Cambridge: Polity Press.

Lundmark, Carina (1995) 'Feminist Political Orientations', in J. van Deth and E. Scarbrough (eds), *The Impact of Values*. Oxford: Oxford University Press.

Lyon, David (1994) *Postmodernity*. Buckingham: Open University Press.

Lyotard, Jean-François (1984) *The Postmodern Condition: A Report on Knowledge*. Manchester: Manchester University Press.

MacDonald, Keith M. (1995) *The Sociology of the Professions*. London: Sage.

McGrew, Tony (1992) 'A Global Society?', in S. Hall, D. Held and T. McGrew (eds), *Modernity and its Futures*. Cambridge: Polity Press.

McGuiness, Barbara (1997) 'Rorty, Literary Narratives and Political Philosophy', *History of the Human Sciences*, 10: 29–44.

McQuail, Denis (1994) *Mass Communication Theory*. 3rd edition. London: Sage.

Maine, Henry (1917) *Ancient Law*. London: Dent.

Marsh, David and Gerry Stoker (eds) (1995) *Theory and Methods in Political Science*. London: Macmillan.

Melucci, Alberto (1980) 'New Social Movements: A Theoretical Approach', *Social Science Information*, 19: 199-226.

Melucci, Alberto (1988) 'Social Movements and the Democratization of Everyday Life', in J. Keane (ed.), *Civil Society and the State*. London: Verso.

Melucci, Alberto (1989) *Nomads of the Present*. London: Hutchinson.

References

Mendus, Susan (1989) *Toleration and the Limits of Liberalism*. London: Macmillan.

Mendus, Susan (1996) 'Some Mistakes in Impartiality', *Political Studies*, 44: 319–327.

Meyrowitz, Joshua (1985) *No Sense of Place: The Impact of Electronic Media on Social Behavior*. New York: Oxford University Press.

Middlemas, Robert (1979) *Politics in Industrial Society: The Experience of the British Political System since 1911*. London: Andre Deutsch.

Milbrath, Lester (1965) *Political Participation*. Chicago: Rand McNally.

Miller, David (1995) 'Citizenship and Pluralism', *Political Studies*, 43: 432–450.

Mills, C. Wright (1959) *The Sociological Imagination*. Oxford: Oxford University Press.

Misztal, Barbara (1996) *Trust in Modern Societies*. Cambridge: Polity Press.

Mitchell, Juliet (1990) *Psychoanalysis and Feminism*. 2nd edition. Harmondsworth: Penguin.

Mohammadi, Ali (ed.) (1997) *International Communication and Globalization*. London: Sage.

Moore, George (1903) *Principia Ethica*. Cambridge: Cambridge University Press.

Moores, Shaun (1988) '"The Box on the Dresser": Memories of Early Radio and Everyday Life', *Media, Culture and Society*, 10: 23–40.

Moores, Shaun (1995) 'Media, Modernity, and Lived Experience', *Journal of Communication Inquiry*, 19: 5–19.

Moores, Shaun (1996) *Satellite Television and Everyday Life: Articulating Technology*. Luton: John Libbey Media.

Morley, David (1986) *Family Television: Cultural Power and Domestic Leisure*. London: Comedia.

Mort, Frank (1989) 'The Politics of Consumption', in S. Hall and M. Jacques (eds), *New Times: The Changing Face of Politics in the 1990s*. London: Lawrence and Wishart.

Mort, Frank (1996) *The Culture of Consumption: Masculinities and Social Space in Late Twentieth-Century Britain*. London: Routledge.

Mouffe, Chantal (1988) 'Radical Democracy: Modern or Postmodern?', in A. Ross (ed.), *Universalism Abandoned? The Politics of Postmodernism*. Minneapolis: University of Minnesota Press.

Mouffe, Chantal (ed.) (1992) *Dimensions of Radical Democracy: Pluralism, Citizenship, Community*. London: Verso.

Mouffe, Chantal (1993) 'Liberal Socialism and Pluralism: Which Citizenship?', in J. Squires (ed.), *Principled Positions*. London: Lawrence and Wishart.

Mulhall, Stephen and Adam Swift (1992) *Liberals and Communitarians*. Oxford: Blackwell.

Murray, Robin (1989) 'Fordism and Post-Fordism', in S. Hall and M. Jacques (eds), *New Times: The Changing Face of Politics in the 1990s*. London: Lawrence and Wishart.

Newcomb, Horace and Paul Hirsch (1987) 'Television as a Cultural Forum', in H. Newcomb (ed.), *Television: The Critical View*. 4th edition. New York: Oxford University Press.

Nicholson, Linda J. (ed.) (1990) *Feminism/Postmodernism*. London: Routledge.

Niedermayer, Oskar and Richard Sinnott (eds) (1995) *Public Opinion and Internationalized Government*. Oxford: Oxford University Press.

Oakeshott, Michael (1933) *Experience and its Modes*. Oxford: Clarendon Press.

O'Connor, James (1973) *The Fiscal Crisis of the State*. New York: St Martin's Press.

O'Connor, James (1984) *Accumulation Crisis*. New York: Blackwell.

Offe, Claus (1984) *Contradictions of the Welfare State*. London: Hutchinson.

Offe, Claus (1985) *Disorganized Capitalism*. Cambridge: Cambridge University Press.

Offe, Claus (1995) *Modernity and the State*. Cambridge: Polity Press.

Oldfield, Adrian (1990) *Citizenship and Community: Civic Republicanism and the Modern World*. London: Routledge.

Orr, Robert (1973) 'The Time Motif in Machiavelli', in M. Fleisher (ed.), *Machiavelli and the Nature of Modern Political Thought*. London: Croom Helm.

Pannwitz, Rudolf (1917) *Die Krisis der Europäischen Kultur*. Nuremberg: Hans Carl.

Parekh, Bhikhu (1993) 'The Cultural Particularity of Liberal Democracy', in D. Held (ed.), *Prospects for Democracy*. Cambridge: Polity Press.

Parekh, Bhikhu (1997) 'Minority Practices and Principles of Toleration', *International Migration Review*, 30: 251–281.

Pekonen, Kyösti (1989) 'Symbols and Politics as Culture in the Modern Situation: The Problem and Prospects of the "New"', in J. Gibbins (ed.), *Contemporary Political Culture: Politics in a Postmodern Age*. London: Sage.

Pettit, Phillip (1997) *Republicanism: A Theory of Freedom and Government*. Oxford: Oxford University Press.

Phillips, Anne (1993) *Democracy and Difference*. Cambridge: Polity Press.

References

Phillips, Anne (1994) 'Pluralism, Solidarity and Change', in J. Weeks (ed.), *The Lesser Evil and the Greater Good*. London: River Oram Press.

Phillips, Anne (1995) *The Politics of Presence*. Oxford: Clarendon.

Pinkney, Robert (1997) 'The Sleeping Night-Watchman and Some Alternatives: Citizenship, Participation and Bases for Democratic Legislation in Britain', *Government and Opposition*, 32: 340–366.

Pocock, John G.A. (1973) *Politics, Language and Time*. New York: Athenaeum.

Pocock, John G.A. (1975) *The Machiavellian Moment*. Princeton: Princeton University Press.

Poster, Mark (1990) *The Mode of Information: Poststructuralism and Social Context*. Cambridge: Polity Press.

Radway, Janice (1984) *Reading the Romance: Women, Patriarchy, and Popular Literature*. London: Verso.

Rawls, John (1993) *Political Liberalism*. New York: Columbia University Press.

Reimer, Bo (1989) 'Postmodern Structures of Feeling. Values and Life Style in the Postmodern Age', in J. Gibbins (ed.), *Contemporary Political Culture: Politics in a Postmodern Age*. London: Sage.

Reimer, Bo (1994) *The Most Common of Practices: On Mass Media Use in Late Modernity*. Stockholm: Almqvist and Wiksell International.

Reimer, Bo (1995) 'The Media in Public and Private Spheres', in J. Fornäs and G. Bolin (eds), *Youth Culture in Late Modernity*. London: Sage.

Reimer, Bo (1997) 'Texts, Contexts, Structures. Audience Studies and the Micro-Macro Link', in U. Carlsson (ed.), *Beyond Media Uses and Effects*. Gothenburg: Nordicom.

Reimer, Bo (1998) 'Diversity and Polarization: On Mediazation Processes in Late Modernity', in H.W. Giessen (ed.), *Long-Term Consequences on Social Structures through Mass Media Impact*. Berlin: Vistas.

Rengger, Nicholas J. (1989) 'Incommensurability, International Theory and the Fragmentation of Western Culture', in J. Gibbins (ed.), *Contemporary Political Culture: Politics in a Postmodern Age*. London: Sage.

Rengger, Nicholas J. (1995) *Political Theory, Modernity and Postmodernity*. Oxford: Blackwell.

Rhodes, Rod A.W. (1996) 'The New Governance: Governing without Government', *Political Studies*, 44: 652–667.

Robertson, Roland (1992) *Globalization. Social Theory and Global Culture*. London: Sage.

Robertson, Roland (1995) 'Glocalization: Time–Space and Homogeneity–Heterogeneity', in M. Featherstone, S. Lash and R. Robertson (eds), *Global Modernities*. London: Sage.

Robertson, Roland and Frank Lechner (1985) 'Modernization, Globalization and the Problem of Culture in World-Systems Theory', *Theory, Culture & Society*, 2: 103–117.

Rorty, Richard (1979) *Philosophy and the Mirror of Nature*. Oxford: Blackwell.

Rorty, Richard (1983) 'Postmodernist Bourgeois Liberalism', *Journal of Philosophy*, 80: 583–589.

Rorty, Richard (1989) *Contingency, Irony and Solidarity*. Cambridge: Cambridge University Press.

Rose, Margaret (1991) *The Post-Modern and the Post-Industrial*. Cambridge: Cambridge University Press.

Rosenau, Pauline Marie (1992) *Post-Modernism and the Social Sciences*. Princeton: Princeton University Press.

Rosenau, James N. and Ernst-Otto Czempiel (1992) *Governance without Government: Order and Change in World Politics*. Cambridge: Cambridge University Press.

Rosengren, Karl Erik, Lawrence A. Wenner and Philip Palmgreen (eds) (1985) *Media Gratifications Research: Current Perspectives*. Beverly Hills: Sage.

Runciman, Walter G. (1972) *Relative Deprivation and Social Justice*. Harmondsworth: Pelican.

Ryan, Michael (1988) *Culture and Politics*. London: Macmillan.

Sandel, Michael (1982) *Liberalism and the Limits of Justice*. Cambridge: Cambridge University Press.

Sandel, Michael (1996) *Democracy's Discontent: America in Search of a Public Policy*. Cambridge, MA: Harvard University Press.

Saunders, Peter (1985) 'Corporatism and Urban Service Provision', in W. Grant (ed.), *The Political Economy of Corporatism*. London: Macmillan.

Scarbrough, Elinor (1995) 'Materialist-Postmaterialist Value Orientations', in J. van Deth and E. Scarbrough (eds), *The Impact of Values*. Oxford: Oxford University Press.

Schiller, Herbert I. (1976) *Communication and Cultural Domination*. New York: M.E. Sharpe.

Schiller, Herbert I. (1996) *Information Inequality: The Deepening Social Crisis in America*. New York: Routledge.

Schmitt, Rüdiger (1989) 'From "Old Politics" to "New Politics": Three Decades of Peace Protest in Western Germany', in J. Gibbins (ed.), *Contemporary Political Culture: Politics in a Postmodern Age*. London: Sage.

References

Schutz, Alfred and Thomas Luckmann (1973) *The Structures of the Life-World*. Evanston, IL: Northwestern University Press.

Searle, John (1967) 'How to Derive "Ought" from "Is"', in P. Foot (ed.), *Theories of Ethics*, Oxford: Oxford University Press.

Segal, Lyn (ed.) (1997) *The New Sexual Agenda*. London: Macmillan.

Seglow, Jonathan (1996) 'Richard Rorty and the Problem of the Person', *Politics*, 16: 39-45.

Seidman, Steven (1998) *Contested Knowledge: Social Theory in the Postmodern Era*. 2nd edition. Oxford: Blackwell.

Seitz, Brian (1995) *The Trace of Political Representation*. Albany: State University of New York Press.

Shields, Rob (1992) *Lifestyle Shopping: The Subject of Consumption*. London: Routledge.

Shildrich, Margrit (1997) *Leaky Bodies and Boundaries: Feminism, Postmodernism and (Bio)Ethics*. London: Routledge.

Silverstone, Roger (1994) *Television and Everyday Life*. London: Routledge.

Smart, Barry (1993) *Postmodernity*. London: Routledge.

Smith, Bernard (1945) *Place, Taste and Tradition*. Oxford: Oxford University Press.

Somervell, D.C. (ed.) (1946) *A Study of History by Arnold J. Toynbee*, Oxford: Oxford University Press.

Soper, Kate (1993) 'Postmodernism, Subjectivity and the Question of Value', in J. Squires (ed.), *Principled Positions: Postmodernism and the Rediscovery of Values*. London: Lawrence and Wishart.

Squires, Judith (ed.) (1993) *Principled Positions: Postmodernism and the Rediscovery of Values*. London: Lawrence and Wishart.

Squires, Judith (1994) 'Ordering the City: Public Space and Political Representation', in J. Weeks (ed.), *The Lesser Evil and the Greater Good*. London: River Oram Press.

Sreberny-Mohammadi, Annabelle (1996) 'The Global and the Local in International Communications', in J. Curran and M. Gurevitch (eds), *Mass Media and Society*. 2nd edition. London: Arnold.

Taylor, Charles (1989) *Sources of the Self: The Making of the Modern Identity*. Cambridge, MA: Harvard University Press.

Tester, Keith (1992) *Civil Society*. London: Routledge.

Theile, Leslie Paul (1997) *Thinking Politics: Perspectives in Ancient, Modern, and Postmodern Political Theory*. Chatham, NJ: Chatham House.

Therborn, Göran (1995a) *European Modernity and Beyond: The Trajectory of European Societies 1945–2000*. London: Sage.

Therborn, Göran (1995b) 'Routes to/Through Modernity', in M.

Featherstone, S. Lash and R. Robertson (eds), *Global Modernities*. London: Sage.

Thompson, Helen (1996) 'The New State and International Capital Flows', *Government and Opposition*, 32: 84–113.

Thompson, John B. (1995) *The Media and Modernity: A Social Theory of the Media*. Cambridge: Polity Press.

Tomlinson, Alan (ed.) (1990) *Consumption, Identity and Style: Marketings, Meanings, and the Packaging of Leisure*. London: Routledge.

Tomlinson, John (1991) *Cultural Imperialism: A Critical Introduction*. Baltimore: Johns Hopkins University Press.

Touraine, Alain (1974) *The Post-Industrial Society*. London: Wildwood House.

Touraine, Alain (1997) *What is Democracy?* Boulder, CO: Westview.

Toynbee, Arnold, J. (1939) *A Study of History*. Vols 1–6. London: Oxford University Press.

Tsagarousianou, Roza, Damien Tambini and Cathy Byran (eds) (1997) *Cyberdemocracy*. London: Routledge.

van Deth, Jan (1995) 'Introduction: The Impact of Values', in J. van Deth and E. Scarbrough (eds), *The Impact of Values*. Oxford: Oxford University Press.

van Deth, Jan and Elinor Scarbrough (eds) (1995) *The Impact of Values*. Oxford: Oxford University Press.

Vattimo, Gianni (1988) *The End of Modernity: Nihilism and Hermeneutics in Post-Modern Culture*. Cambridge: Polity Press.

Vattimo, Gianni (1992) *The Transparent Society*. Cambridge: Polity Press.

Veblen, Thorstein (1899/1949) *The Theory of the Leisure Class*. London: George Allen and Unwin.

Virilio, Paul (1990) *L'Inertie polaire*. Paris: Christian Bourgeois.

Walzer, Michael (1983) *Spheres of Justice*. Oxford: Martin Robertson.

Walzer, Michael (1997) *On Tolerance*, London: Yale University Press.

Waters, Malcolm (1995) *Globalization*. London: Routledge.

Weber, Cynthia (1994) *Simulating Sovereignty: Intervention, the State and Symbolic Exchange*. Cambridge: Cambridge University Press.

Weber, Max (1968) *Economy and Society*. New York: Free Press.

Weeks, Jeffrey (1993) 'Rediscovering Values', in J. Squires (ed.), *Principled Positions: Postmodernism and the Rediscovery of Values*. London: Lawrence and Wishart.

Weeks, Jeffrey (1995) *Invented Moralities: Sexual Values in an Age of Uncertainty*. Cambridge: Polity Press.

Weintraub, Jeff and Krishan Kumar (eds) (1997) *Public and Private in*

References

Thought and Practice. London: University of Chicago Press.

White, Stephen (1993) *Political Theory and Postmodernism*. Cambridge: Cambridge University Press.

Williams, Raymond (1961) *The Long Revolution: An Analysis of the Democratic, Industrial and Cultural Changes Transforming Our Society*. London: Chatto and Windus.

Winch, Peter (1974) 'Understanding a Primitive Society', in B. Wilson (ed.), *Rationality*. Oxford: Blackwell.

Wittgenstein, Ludwig (1958) *Philosophical Investigations*. Oxford: Blackwell.

Witz, Anne (1992) *Professions and Patriarchy*. London: Routledge.

Yeatman, Anna (1994) *Postmodern Revisionings of the Political*. London: Routledge.

Young, Iris Marion (1990) *Justice and the Politics of Difference*. Princeton: Princeton University Press.

Young, Iris Marion (1993) 'Together in Difference: Transforming the Logic of Group Political Conflict', in J. Squires (ed.), *Principled Positions: Postmodernism and the Rediscovery of Values*. London: Lawrence and Wishart.

Yturbe, Corina (1997) 'On Norberto Bobbio's Theory of Democracy', *Political Theory*, 25: 377–400.

Ziehe, Thomas (1986) *Ny ungdom: Om ovanliga läroprocesser*. Stockholm: Norstedts.

Name Index

Index

Index

Index

Subject Index

199

Index

200

Index

Index

Index